# HIGHER ECONOMICS

## COURSE REVISION NOTES AND QUESTIONS

# DUNCAN McMASTER

# DISCLAIMER

Every effort has been made to ensure that the content provided in this book is accurate and helpful to the readers at publishing time. The author/publisher cannot accept responsibility for any loss, negative impact or outcome based on errors or omissions made within this publication.

# Contents

# INTRODUCTION

Welcome to this guide which provides course revision notes and questions for the Higher Economics Course from the Scottish Qualifications Authority (SQA).

The SQA Higher Economics course consists of 3 areas of study –

➢ Economics of the Market

➢ UK Economic Activity

➢ Global Economic Activity

There are two parts to the external assessment – an assignment and a question paper. These notes will help prepare you for the question paper element which carries 75% of the overall mark.

The Question Paper has 2 sections, 90 marks and takes 2 hours 30 minutes to complete.

Section 1 – 30 marks and contains two 15 mark multi-part questions (range between 1-4 marks)

Section 2 – 60 marks and contains three 20 mark multi-part questions (range between 2-8 marks)

Websites to help with your studies:

www.sqa.org.uk – contains course syllabus, past papers and solutions.

www.scholar.ac.uk – notes and questions created by Heriot-Watt University. All schools signed up for this should provide pupils with a username and 7-character password to access site.

www.understandingstandards.org.uk – SQA site containing previous pupils scripts to help understand the marking process.

www.dineshbakshi.com – some revision quizzes although not written for the SQA syllabus - the closest course to use on the site is IB Economics.

# TRENDS

In the final exam knowledge of, and reasons for, the trend in the rates of and inflation, GDP, unemployment and imports and exports over the previous year could be asked.

Past paper solutions relating to questions on trends may not apply to the current situation and care should be taken over this.

It will be necessary to find information on rates before the exam and websites such as www.trading economics.com will provide this data. It is not necessary to memorise every monthly figure but rather know the most recent rates and the trend that is taking place.

A trend is a general direction in which something is developing or changing

When describing trends the following wordings could be used:

- ➢ Rate or amount has increased/decreased and reached its highest/lowest in xx

- ➢ Rate or amount is currently at xx

- ➢ Rate or figure has increased/decreased steadily from xx to yy

- ➢ Rate has fluctuated over the last year but is now at xx which is higher/lower than 12 months ago

- ➢ Rate or figure is below/above target (for inflation)

- ➢ Rate or figure is at its lowest/highest for many years or since xx

# UNIT ONE – ECONOMICS OF THE MARKET

# THE BASIC ECONOMIC PROBLEM

The reason for the study of economics is, to understand better and create solutions to help with, the basic economic problem which is ultimately impossible to solve.

The basic economic problem is scarcity.

Economic resources of land, labour and capital are used to make goods and provide services that people want and need. However, these resources (land, labour and capital) are scarce (limited) and individuals' wants and needs are unlimited due to greed and technical advances.

## Choice and Opportunity cost

Due to scarcity, choices have to be made by individuals, businesses and government on how best to use the limited resources they have.

When choices are made by individuals, businesses or government alternatives are given up or sacrificed.

The opportunity cost of a decision is the value of the next best alternative that is not chosen.

Examples –

➢ the opportunity cost of a family spending £10,000 on a holiday is the new car they cannot purchase with that £10,000.

➢ the opportunity cost of a government spending £1 million on building a new hospital is the new school that can't be built with that £1 million.

# Economic and Free Goods

Virtually all goods and services are scarce and are called economic goods. Those that are not scarce are called free goods.

- ➢ Economic goods are goods that carry a price whereas free goods do not command a price.

- ➢ Free goods use up no scare resources in production whereas economic goods do use up scarce resources.

- ➢ Free goods create no opportunity cost whereas economic goods do incur an opportunity cost.

# Economic Systems

The economic problem of scarcity creates the following questions:

> ➢ What goods and services should an economy produce?

> ➢ How should goods and services be produced?

> ➢ Who should receive the goods and services that are produced?

There are broadly three types of economic system which attempt to answer these questions.

## 1 - Command/Planned Economy

In a command or planned economy the government are in complete control of how resources are allocated and they own all the resources. Every worker is therefore in the public sector as no private sector exists.

This system was often found in communist nations and the UK had a planned economy during World War 2.

This system redistributes income and wealth equally so that all people are the same, believing that if resources are owned by private individuals this leads to inequality.

### Answering the questions in a command/planned economy

> ➢ What to produce? – decided by the government planners who estimate what they think the population needs.

> ➢ How to produce? – government sets requirements for each factory and allocates the necessary resources.

> ➢ Who receives? – prices and incomes are controlled by the government so that every member of society receives the same.

## 2 - Free Market Economy

In a free market economy consumers and businesses would deal with the basic economic problem. Every worker is in the private sector as no public sector exists.

All resources are allocated by a PRICE MECHANISM using market forces of demand (from consumers) and supply (from businesses) to set the price – covered in more detail later in this area of study.

The PRICE MECHANISM involves the following steps:

➢ Demand comes from consumers and an increase in demand will cause a shortage and raise the price.

➢ If prices rise then the good or service becomes more profitable meaning more businesses will seek to produce that product.

➢ More resources are required to make the product in order to supply more.

➢ Resources are then reallocated to the production of more profitable products and away from less profitable ones.

➢ No country has a completely free market economy and a government always has to be involved.

## Answering the questions in a free market economy

> What to produce? – decided by consumers - what they demand will be produced by businesses.

> How to produce? – decided by the producer – businesses will use the most efficient methods of production in order to keep costs down and make as much profit as possible.

> Who receives? – in theory goods and services are available to all consumers but in reality only to those with enough income to afford the prices being charged.

## 3 - Mixed economy

In a mixed economy the private sector and the public sector (government) work together in order to meet the needs and wants of a country.

All countries in the world are mixed but some are closer to the command system, with the government in control of more resources and other countries closer to the free market with the price mechanism being the way in which resources are allocated for many goods and services.

In the 1980s the UK moved more to the free market with the privatisation of many government owned businesses like British Telecom, British Gas, British Airways and British Rail.

# MARKET INTERVENTION

In a mixed economy a government exists and intervenes to prevent/correct market failure by creating rules, laws and providing subsidies or grants.

Market Failure occurs when the private sector of the economy fails to supply the type and/or quantity of goods and services required by consumers.

## Methods or examples of market failure/Disadvantages of a free market economy/Problems with the price mechanism/Reasons for government intervention

All the different wordings shown above indicate the various ways a question could be worded but the answer to each is exactly the same. This section gives reasons why there has to be some form of government in an economy.

### 1 - No public goods

Public goods are goods and services that would not be provided in a free market by the workings of the price mechanism because businesses/entrepreneurs would not be able to charge for them because they are:

> ➢ Non-excludable – once the goods are provided it is not possible to exclude people from using them even if they have not paid. This allows free riders to consume goods without paying any money for them.

> ➢ Non-rival – this means that the consumption of the good by one person doesn't diminish the amount available for the next person.

Public goods would not exist in a free market economy.

## 2 - Not enough merit goods

Merit goods are goods and services which are considered desirable for all in a country to receive but in a free market not all people would be able to afford them if asked to pay and would therefore not consume or purchase them.

Merit goods would exist in a free market economy and are available in a mixed economy by private sector businesses but only to those who choose to pay.

## 3 - Too many demerit goods

Demerit goods are goods and services which are considered harmful to society. These goods and services are very profitable to entrepreneurs/businesses and would be over consumed in a free market economy without a government to monitor their use.

## 4 - Negative and positive externalities would be uncontrolled

A negative externality occurs when everyone in society faces additional costs over and above those incurred by a business who would not consider these costs when setting their price.

A positive externality occurs when consumers that do not actually purchase a product receive some benefit.

## 5 - Income inequalities

The gap between rich and poor would be unlimited in a completely free market economy. Many argue there are significant inequalities in many mixed economies in the world today but it would be even worse without a government to provide basic pensions and benefits to the unemployed.

## 6 - Lack of competition

In a free market economy businesses could become too large and powerful and have less need to keep prices down and quality high.

These larger businesses would be able to use destroyer pricing, where prices are set below cost, to eliminate competitors.

Cartels would develop between businesses – a cartel is a group of businesses who agree not to compete with each other.

# Ways a government intervenes to correct or reduce market failure

Legislation (laws) can be introduced by governments in order to:

> Redistribute wealth and reduce income inequality.

> Reduce negative externalities.

> Reduce consumption of demerit goods.

The government may also provide through taxation:

> Public goods – goods not provided in a free market.

> Transfer payments – benefits and pensions to ensure a minimum living standard for the population.

> Merit goods – goods that provide a social benefit.

Governments can prevent businesses becoming too large by using legislation and in the UK it has created the Competition and Markets Authority.

## Private goods

Effectively private goods are the opposite of public goods. Note these are not a reason for market failure.

Private goods are goods which businesses can restrict to those who pay for them. Once the good is bought the consumer will be the only one who receives the benefit. They therefore have a rival and are excludable.

# PRODUCTION POSSIBILITY DIAGRAMS/CURVES/FRONTIERS

Production Possibility Diagrams are used to demonstrate 3 important concepts in economics:

➢ Opportunity cost - this requires one curve with two points plotted on the curve.

➢ Economic efficiency - this requires one curve and one point plotted on the curve.

➢ Economic growth - this requires two curves to be drawn.

A Production Possibility Diagram shows the combination of goods and services that can be produced in a country with a given amount of resources.

It simplifies reality and assumes a country is only capable of producing 2 goods or services.

➢ There is no ideal point on a curve as any point on the curve means resources are being used efficiently.

➢ Any point inside the curve would mean resources are not being used efficiently.

➢ Any point outside the curve is not achievable with the current level of resources.

# Production Possibility Diagram showing Opportunity Cost

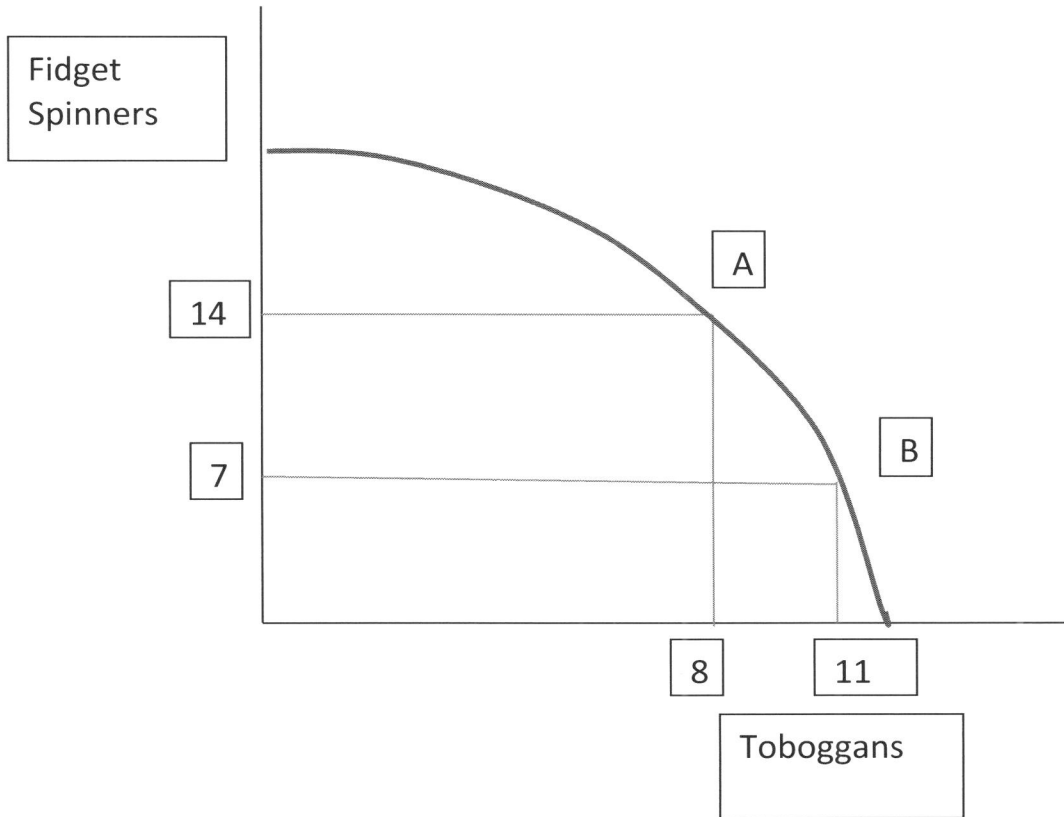

The numbers used and goods shown are for example purposes and any 2 products and appropriate numbers would be fine.

> ➢ Assume a country can produce two goods with its resources – fidget spinners and toboggans.

> ➢ If the country is at point A on the diagram above, it can produce a combination of 14 fidget spinners and 8 toboggans.

> ➢ If it reallocates resources (moving around the PPC from A to B) it can now make 11 toboggans but only 7 fidget spinners.

> ➢ The opportunity cost therefore of gaining 3 more toboggans is losing 7 fidget spinners.

# Production Possibility Diagram showing Economic Efficiency

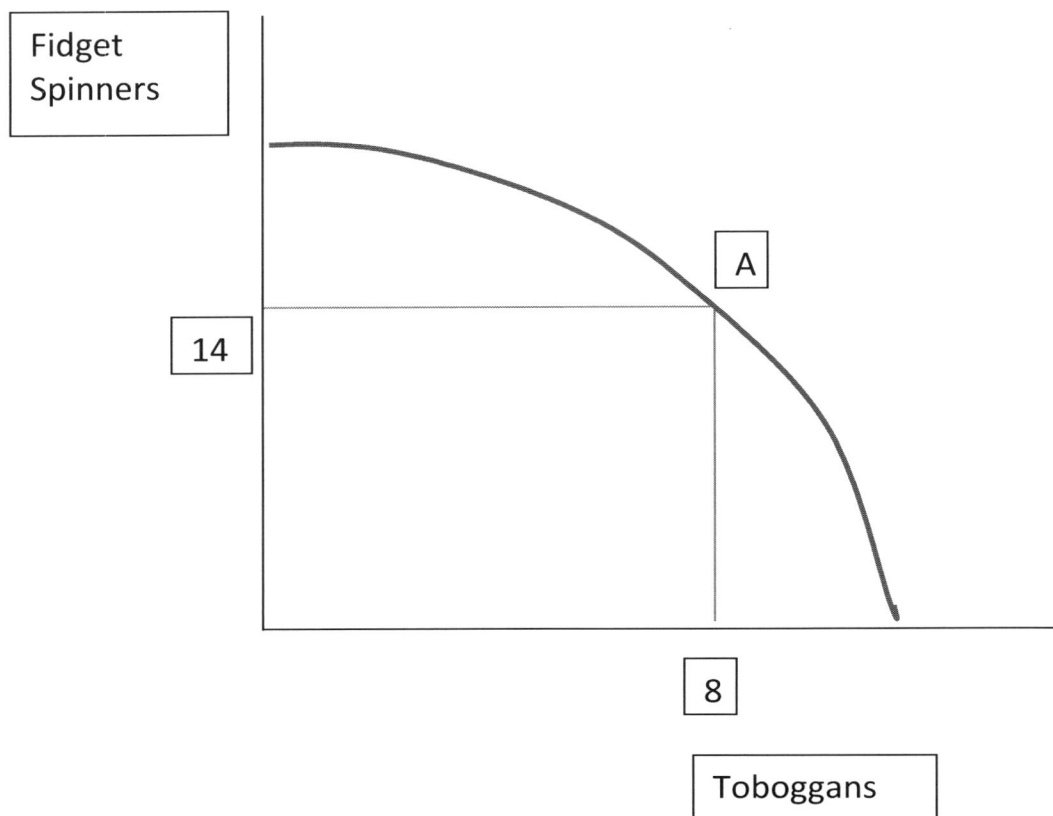

At any point on the curve technical efficiency exists but only a single point (A) illustrates economic efficiency as this shows the desired combination of the 2 products.

Other combinations on the curve do not show economic efficiency as they indicate what it is possible to achieve with the resources but not what the people of the country wish to be produced.

# Production Possibility Diagram showing Economic Growth

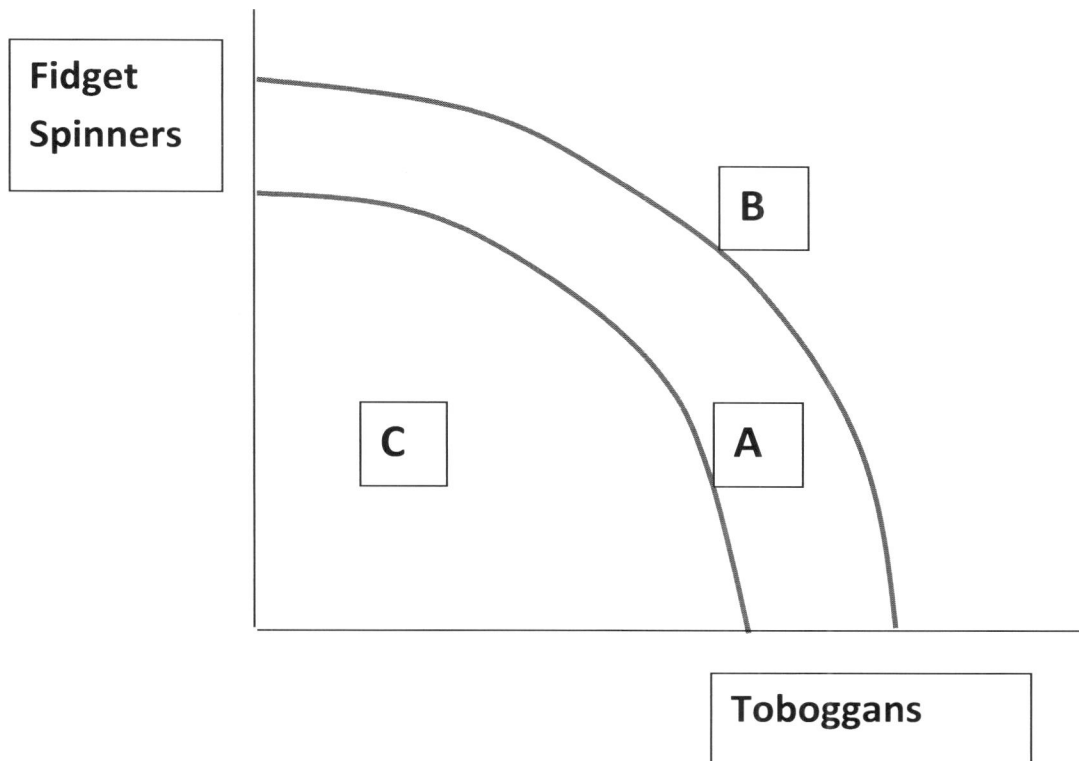

If an economy is producing at any point inside the curve, for example point C, this shows that a country is not using all its resources and is linked to unemployment.

A country can only produce at points outside the curve if it finds a way of expanding its resources or improves the productivity of the resources it already has. This will push the PPC further outwards and indicates economic growth has occurred.

This shift to the right could be achieved if there is:

➤ an increase in the quantity of a nation's resources e.g. more immigration or more babies being born.

➤ an increase in the quality and efficiency of resources e.g. better trained workers.

# Efficiency

Economic efficiency occurs when scarce resources (land, labour, capital) are being best used to produce what people demand and is only achieved when:

> There is productive (technical) efficiency – when the least possible resources are used to make each product i.e. when goods are produced at lowest opportunity cost. Any point on a production possibility curve shows technical efficiency but not necessarily economic efficiency.

> There is allocative efficiency – when the resources are being used to make the products people in the country most want.

When both technical and allocative efficiency are achieved there is economic efficiency.

# DEMAND

Scarce resources are allocated using the price mechanism for many goods and services in a mixed economy.

As mentioned earlier in this guide in a free market prices are determined through the interaction of demand from consumers and supply from businesses. We will now look at each in turn.

Demand – the amount consumers are willing and able to purchase at any given price

## Demand Curve

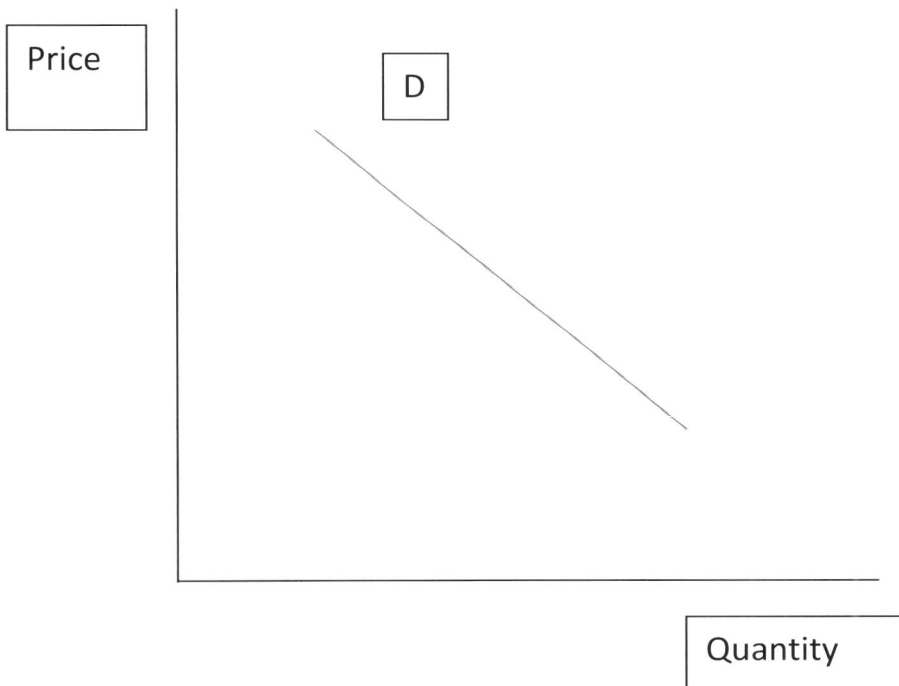

The demand curve slopes downward from left to right indicating an inverse relationship between price and quantity.

The law of demand states that as price falls the quantity demanded rises and as price rises then quantity demanded will fall.

# Slope of normal demand curve

There are three reasons to explain the slope of the normal demand curve:

## Income effect

➢ If prices increase consumers will be able to buy a smaller number of good with the income they have.

➢ This means that their real (adjusted for inflation) income falls and a consumer will react by buying less of a good.

## Substitution effect

➢ As the price of goods increase people are likely to switch and purchase from other businesses instead.

## Law of Diminishing Marginal Utility

➢ Utility means satisfaction or usefulness and a consumer gains utility when they purchase a good or service.

➢ Marginal utility is the utility gained from consuming an extra unit of a good.

➢ Whilst total utility will continue to increase, the law of diminishing marginal utility states that the marginal utility will decline as consumption of a good increases and less satisfaction is gained.

➢ Due to this law, consumers will only be tempted to buy more of a product if the price is lower.

# Abnormal /upward sloping demand curve

There is an argument that for certain goods people actually buy more of them as the price rises.

This goes against the law of demand and would result in an upward sloping demand curve from left to right.

Reasons for the abnormal demand curve include Veblen goods, Giffen goods and Speculative goods.

## Veblen Goods

- ➢ Veblen goods were named after the economist Thorstein Veblen.

- ➢ These are luxury products whose price does not follow the usual laws of demand. Items such as expensive wines, watches and cars become more desirable as they increase in price.

## Speculative Goods

- ➢ Speculative goods are products that are bought even when they rise in price because there is a possibility that they could continue to rise further in price and therefore can be sold at a later date for a profit.

## Giffen Goods

- ➢ Giffen goods were named after the economist Sir Robert Giffen.

- ➢ These are cheaper products whose price may not follow the usual laws of demand. As prices of these products increase consumers, on very limited budgets, purchase more of them as they are unable to afford alternative items.

# Shifts in the demand curve

A contraction or extension of demand is caused by a change in price and results in a movement on a demand curve.

If there is no change in price but the quantity demanded increases or decreases this requires a new demand curve to be drawn to the left or the right of the existing one. Any change in price can be shown on the existing demand curve.

# Factors which causes a shift in the demand curve (determinants of demand)

> Changes in the price of a substitute good - a substitute good is an alternative product which could be purchased so when the price of a substitute good increases that should cause an increase in demand for the alternative product. Any 2 substitute goods are said to have competitive demand.

> Changes in the price of a complimentary good - a complimentary good is one that can be bought in conjunction with others so a rise in the price of a complementary good should cause a fall in demand for a product. Any 2 complementary goods have joint demand.

> Changes in the income of consumers - for most goods when people's income increases the product will be bought in greater quantities and vice versa.

> Changes in fashion - any change due to trends, reputations and fashions.

> Changes in population - an increase in population is likely to cause an increase in demand for goods and services.

> Marketing/advertising - the amount and success of promotions and advertising campaigns will affect consumer demand.

# PRICE ELASTICITY OF DEMAND

Price Elasticity of Demand (Ped) – measures the responsiveness of demand to a change in price. This is how much demand will change following a price movement.

Note that the law of demand tells us demand will fall if the price rises but elasticity is concerned with how much it will fall and the impact this will have on sales revenue.

Sales revenue or just revenue is Price x Quantity Sold.

Formula for Ped =   % change in quantity demanded

_____

% change in price

> If the answer is between 0 and 1, then the product is classed as having inelastic demand and this means the % change in demand is less than the % change in price.

> If the answer is between 1 and infinity, then the product is classed as having elastic demand and this means the % change in demand is greater than the % change in price.

> If the answer is 1 this is classed as unit elasticity and this means that any % change in demand will cause the same % change in price and therefore revenue would be unchanged.

Note that because price and quantity move in different directions the answer will always be a negative number which is largely ignored.

# Factors which determine the price elasticity of demand

> ➢ The number of substitutes for a good or service – the more substitutes the more elastic the demand as even a small change in price will cause many customers to buy an alternative product and demand will fall significantly.

> ➢ The degree of necessity – products that are seen as necessary or are addictive items tend to have inelastic demand and continue to be purchased by most consumers even if price rises significantly.

> ➢ Luxuries – luxuries will tend to be more elastic in demand following a price change as they are more easily given up by people if they become more expensive.

> ➢ Goods which are subject to habitual (regular) consumption tend to be more inelastic as less likely to notice the price changes e.g. loaf of bread.

> ➢ Breadth of definition of a good or service – if a good is broadly defined e.g. fuel then the demand for fuel is fairly inelastic due to it being a necessity but specific brands like fuel from ASDA or fuel from ESSO are likely to be more elastic given the large number of substitutes.

# Importance of Price Elasticity of Demand

Businesses need to know about elasticity of demand as it helps determine whether they should be increasing or decreasing their prices in order to increase their sales revenue.

Government need to know about elasticity to determine what to tax and whether to increase or decrease tax to bring in more revenue. The government tends to tax items which have inelastic demand.

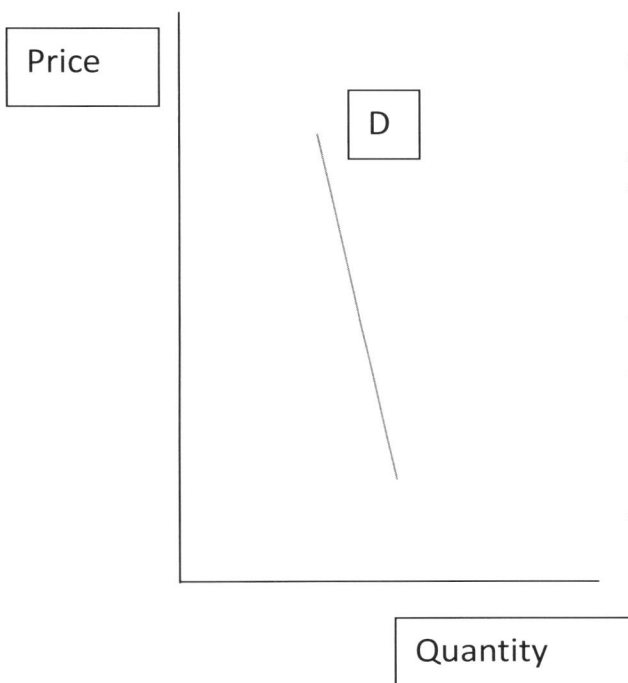

Price

D

Quantity

Diagram to left shows inelastic demand – a steeper demand curve.

Any increase in price will be greater than the fall in demand this causes e.g. a 10% rise in price causes a 5% fall in demand.

Therefore, if a product has inelastic demand the price should be increased to raise sales revenue.

Any fall in price will create a smaller increase in demand and therefore reduce sales revenue.

Price

D

Quantity

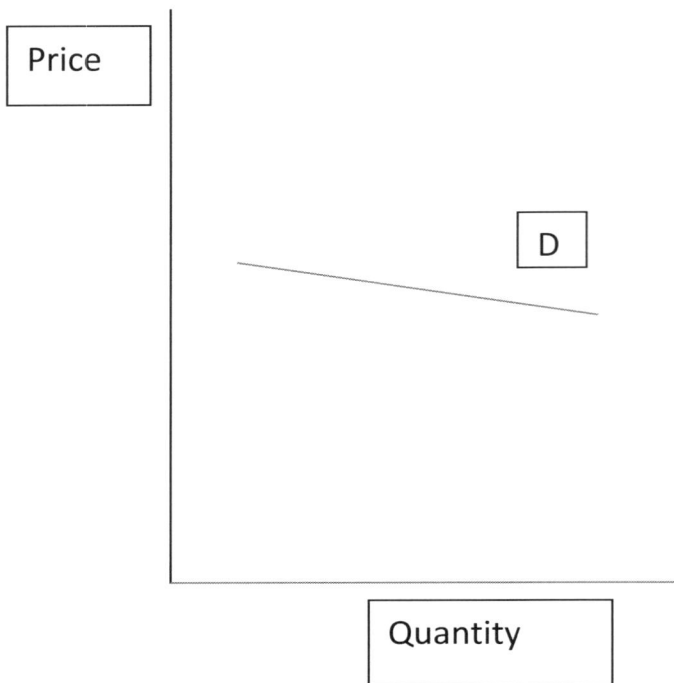

Diagram to left shows elastic demand – a flatter demand curve.

Any increase in price will be smaller than the fall in demand this causes. E.g. a 10% rise in price causes a 50 % fall in demand.

Therefore, if a product has elastic demand the price should be reduced to raise sales revenue.

Any rise in price will create an even greater decrease in demand and therefore reduce sales revenue.

# SUPPLY

Supply is the quantity of a good or service that a seller (business) is willing and able to supply at a given price.

Supply curves slope in an opposite direction to normal demand curve i.e. upwards from left to right.

## Supply Curve

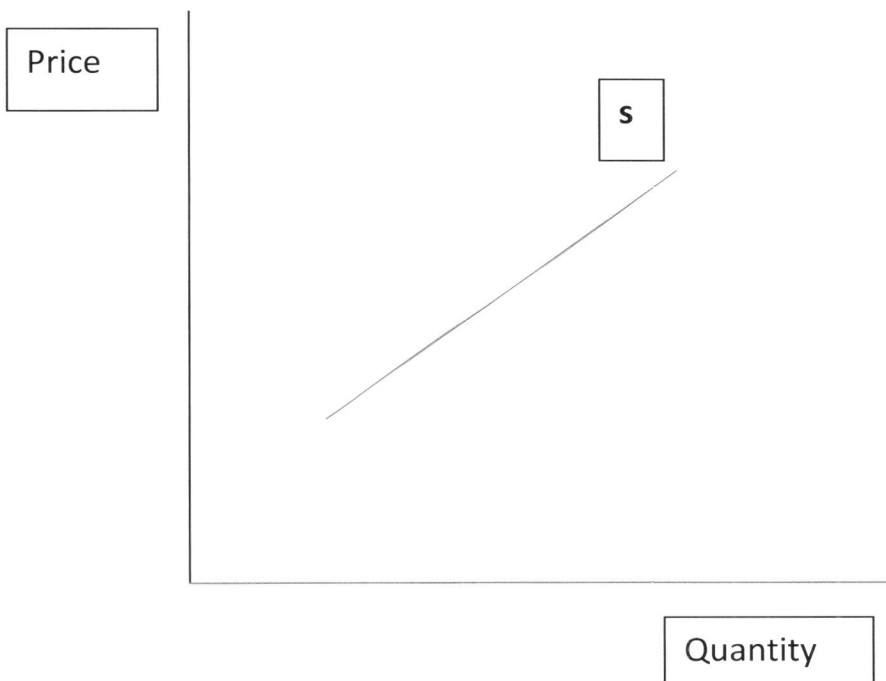

The supply curve slopes upwards from left to right indicating a positive relationship between supply and price. As price rises it encourages producers to offer more products for sale.

## Factors which cause a shift in the supply curve (determinants of supply)

➢ Costs of production – lower costs mean a business can supply more at each price. However, if costs increase the curve will move to the left (less always to the left).

➢ Improvements in technology - Industries where technological change is rapid will cause an increase in supply and a shift to the right.

➢ Government taxes – a change in a tax on businesses will impact cost. If tax increases, then the curve shifts to the left and if tax decreases the curve shifts to the right. Note it is only taxes on business which shift supply whereas changes to taxes on people's income shift demand.

➢ Government subsidies – government assistance to businesses and if they are introduced or increased the will shift the supply curve to the right.

# SETTING THE MARKET PRICE

## What is a market?

This is a place where buyers and sellers come together to exchange goods and services for a price.

## Equilibrium Price and Quantity

➢ Equilibrium occurs where the demand curve and the supply curve cross.

➢ At the point where they cross the price and quantity in a free market is set.

➢ Above equilibrium price supply exceeds demand and there is a surplus and below the equilibrium price demand will exceed supply and there is a shortage.

## Market Diagrams

Diagram showing equilibrium price and quantity

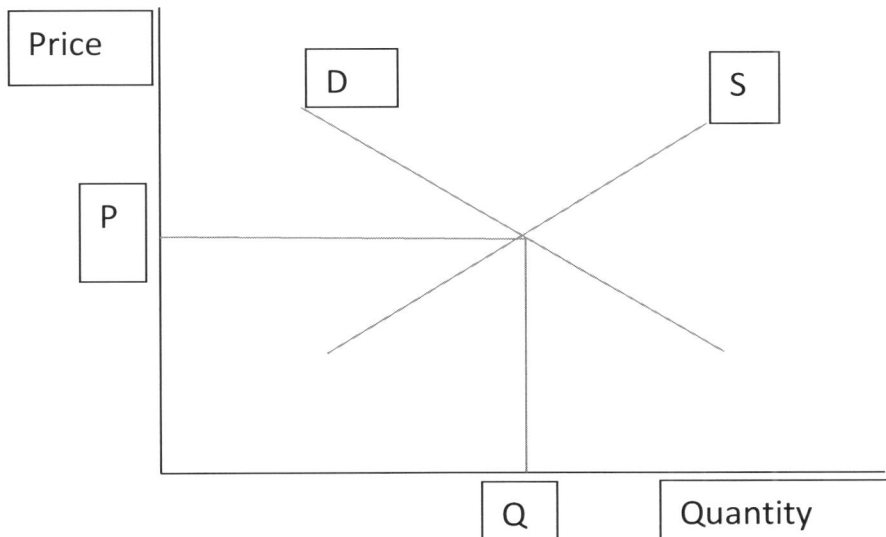

**Diagram showing an increase in demand resulting in a new higher equilibrium price and higher quantity at P1 and Q1**

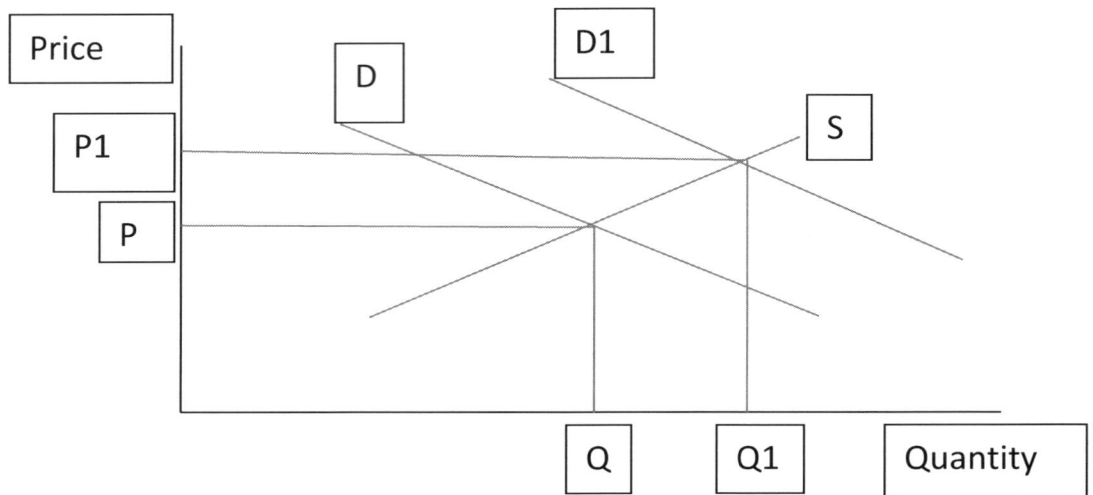

**Diagram showing an increase in supply resulting in a new lower equilibrium price and higher quantity at P1 and Q1**

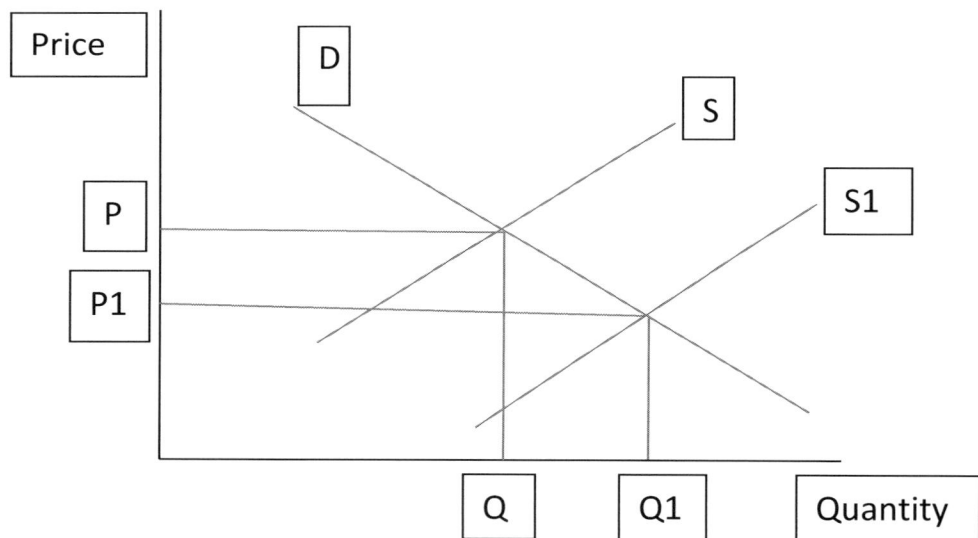

**Diagram showing a reduction in supply resulting in a new higher equilibrium price and lower quantity at P1 and Q1**

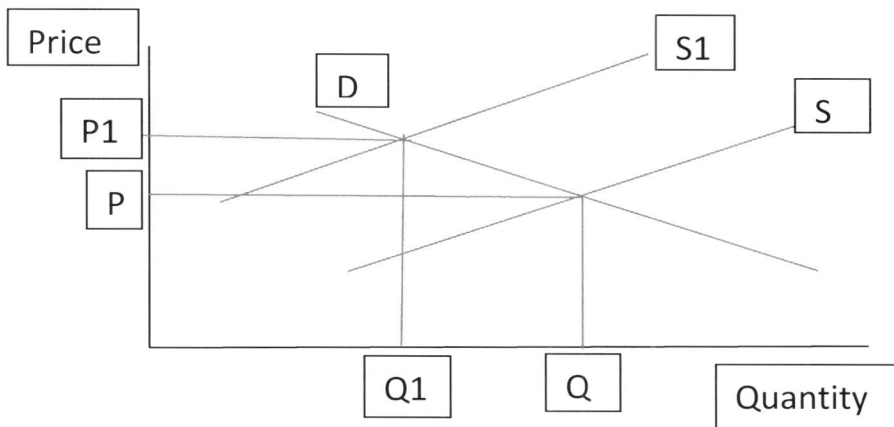

Price
D
S1
S
P1
P
Q1
Q
Quantity

**Diagram showing a reduction in demand resulting in a new lower equilibrium price and lower quantity at P1 and Q1**

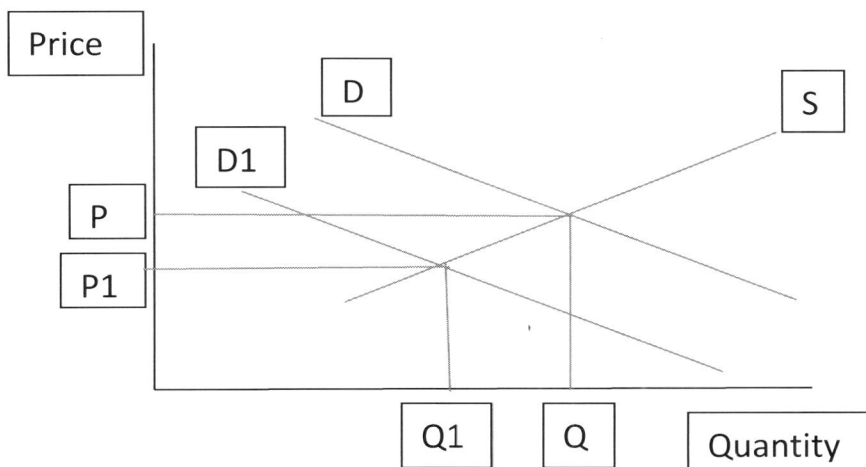

Price
D
D1
S
P
P1
Q1
Q
Quantity

**Diagram showing a reduction in supply and a reduction in demand resulting in a new price P1 and lower quantity at P1 and Q1**

Note the new price is higher simply because the distance between the supply curves is wider than the demand curves.

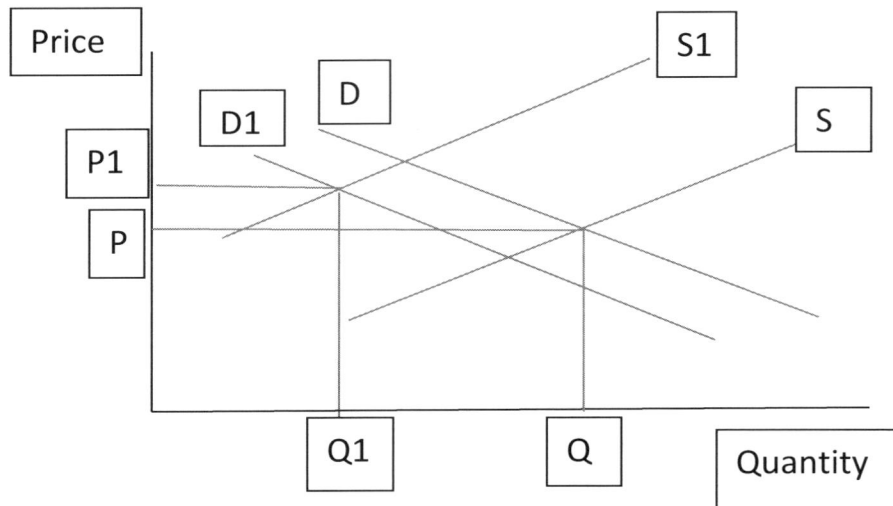

Price | S1 | D | D1 | S | P1 | P | Q1 | Q | Quantity

**Diagram showing a reduction in demand and increase in supply resulting in a new lower equilibrium price and same quantity at P1 and Q1**

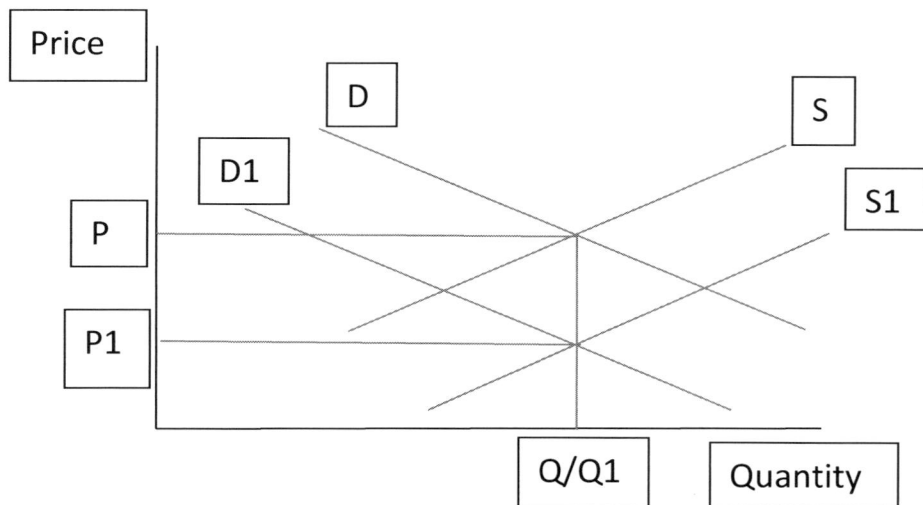

Price | D | S | D1 | S1 | P | P1 | Q/Q1 | Quantity

# Government Intervention – Min and Max Prices

## Minimum Price above equilibrium

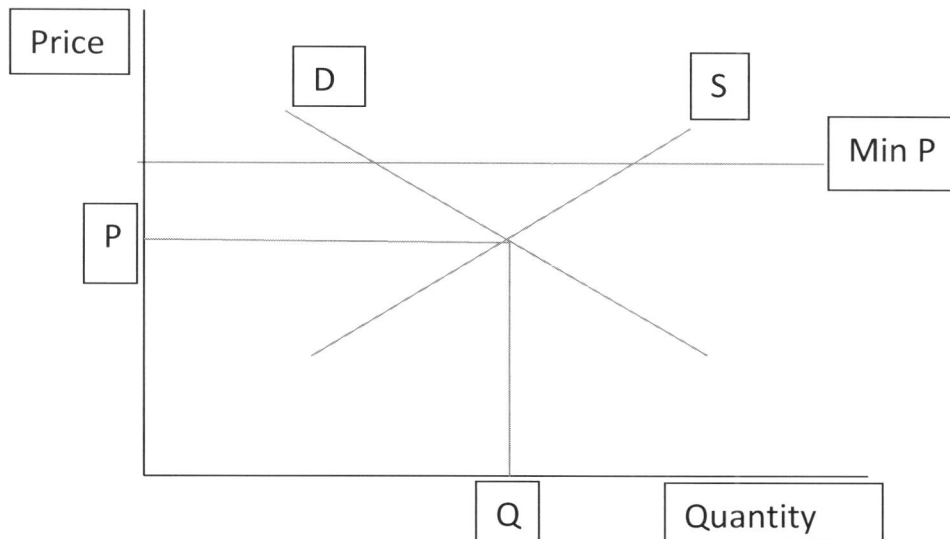

Price

D

S

Min P

P

Q

Quantity

The government can intervene in the free market by increasing or decreasing tax or subsidies (these shift the supply curve) or setting laws on the maximum or minimum price that can be charged for a product.

In the diagram above, a government has imposed a minimum price above the equilibrium that businesses are unable to charge below – e.g. the minimum wage or unit price of alcohol.

At the higher price, demand would be less and supply would be more creating a surplus.

## Maximum Price below equilibrium

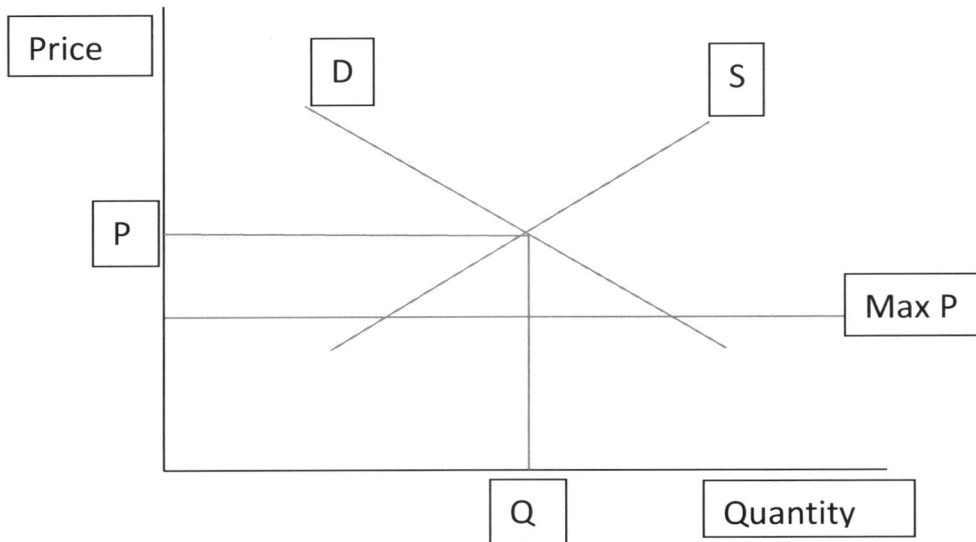

In the diagram above a government has imposed a maximum price below the market price e.g. medical prescription charge.

Businesses reduce the amount offered for sale but customers demand would rise creating a shortage.

Shortages may lead to rationing or illegal prices higher than the free market level.

# COSTS OF PRODUCTION

Before a business will supply any products at a price they must cover their costs of production.

There are 2 time periods to consider when studying costs – the short run and the long run and both will be looked at below.

## Short run time period

This is the time period when at least one factor of production (land, labour capital) is fixed.

Note earlier in the unit we referred to Land, Labour and Capital as resources and now as Factors of Production.

## Fixed costs

> Fixed costs do not change as production or sales (output) increases.

> Fixed costs include rent and bank interest.

> Fixed costs are shown on a diagram as a horizontal straight line.

> If there is no output the Fixed costs are the same as the total costs.

## Variable costs

> Variable costs change directly with output.

> Variable costs include purchases of stock or raw materials.

> Where there is no output there are no variable costs.

## Total Costs (TC) are fixed and variable costs added together.

There are in reality a number of costs which vary with output but not directly called semi variable costs but it is not required to consider these for this course.

## Average Fixed Costs (AFC)

> Average Fixed Cost = Total Fixed Costs/Output.

As fixed costs remain the same in the short run, when output increases, total fixed costs are spread over a larger and larger number of units.

This means that average fixed cost (fixed cost per unit) falls continuously.

## Average Variable Costs (AVC)

> Average Variable Cost = Total Variable Costs/Output.

Whilst total variable costs always rise the average variable costs initially fall then rise.

When average variable costs are falling there are increasing returns to the fixed factor of production.

At some point diminishing returns set in and variable costs per unit will rise.

## Average (Total) Costs (AC)

> Average Cost/Average Total Cost = Total Cost/Output or AFC+AVC=AC.

Average cost is high when output is small then as output increases average cost begins to fall but then begin to rise creating a U shaped curve.

When average costs are falling there are increasing returns to the fixed factor of production due to spreading fixed overheads across more output.

When average costs start rising this is due to diminishing returns to the fixed factor of production.

# Marginal Costs

> ➤ Marginal cost is how much total costs change when output is changed by one unit.

The marginal cost curve cuts the average total cost and average variable cost curves at their lowest points.

The Marginal Cost curve takes the form of a J shape.

Note that in an exam no more than 2 and usually only 1 of the curves shown below will need to be drawn per question.

## Short Run Cost Curves

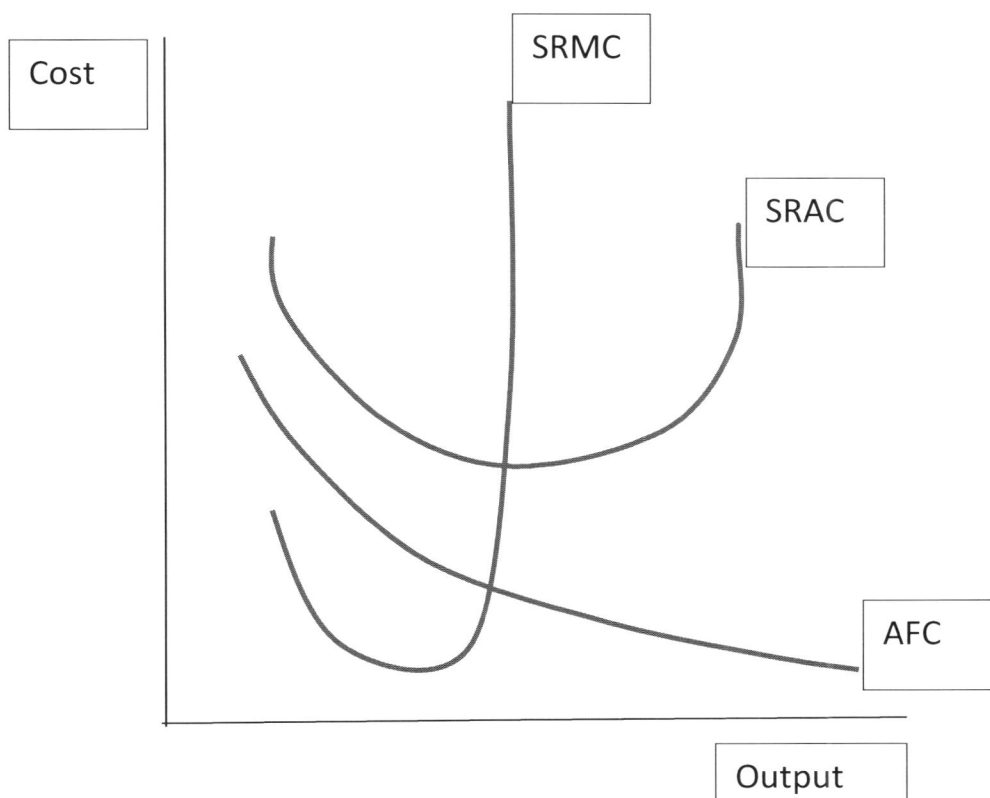

# Law of Increasing and Diminishing Returns

This law explains the shape of the average variable, average total and marginal cost curves in the short run only.

This law states that as more of a variable factor of production e.g. labour, is added to a fixed factor of production e.g. land, then output initially increases but will eventually fall (diminish) as staff numbers become too large and the fixed factor is 'overworked'.

> ➤ Average (total) costs fall due to increasing average returns and rise due to diminishing average returns.

> ➤ Marginal costs fall due to increasing marginal returns and rise due to diminishing marginal returns.

This law and all costs so far apply in the short run time period when at least one factor of production is fixed e.g. land.

In the long run time period there are no fixed costs (all factors of production are variable) and is looked at in the next section.

## Example

If only one member of staff is employed in a hairdressing salon with four booths, then the number of haircuts (output) will be lower than it could be as three booths are unused.

If more staff are employed, then more booths will be used and output should increase but this increased output cannot continue indefinitely.

This would be because there are not enough booths or space if you continue to employ more and more staff as one factor of production (land) is fixed. Each new worker would still need to be paid so although costs per unit fall initially they will rise beyond a certain level of output.

# Short run shut down conditions

If the price a business charges for a product is less than average total cost then it is losing money, however:

➤ Fixed costs must be paid regardless of output.

➤ A business will therefore continue to produce in the short run as long as the price charged is greater than average variable cost.

➤ Staying open can ensure customer loyalty and keep workers from leaving as changes are being made.

➤ If the price is less than average variable cost the business produces zero and closes.

➤ In the long run a firm must cover all costs.

# Long run time period

The long run is the time period when all factors of production (land, labour, capital) are variable so there are no fixed costs.

## Long run average cost curve (LRAC)

The LRAC curve falls due to economies of scale and is made up of a number of short run average cost curves.

The LRAC curve rises due to diseconomies of scale.

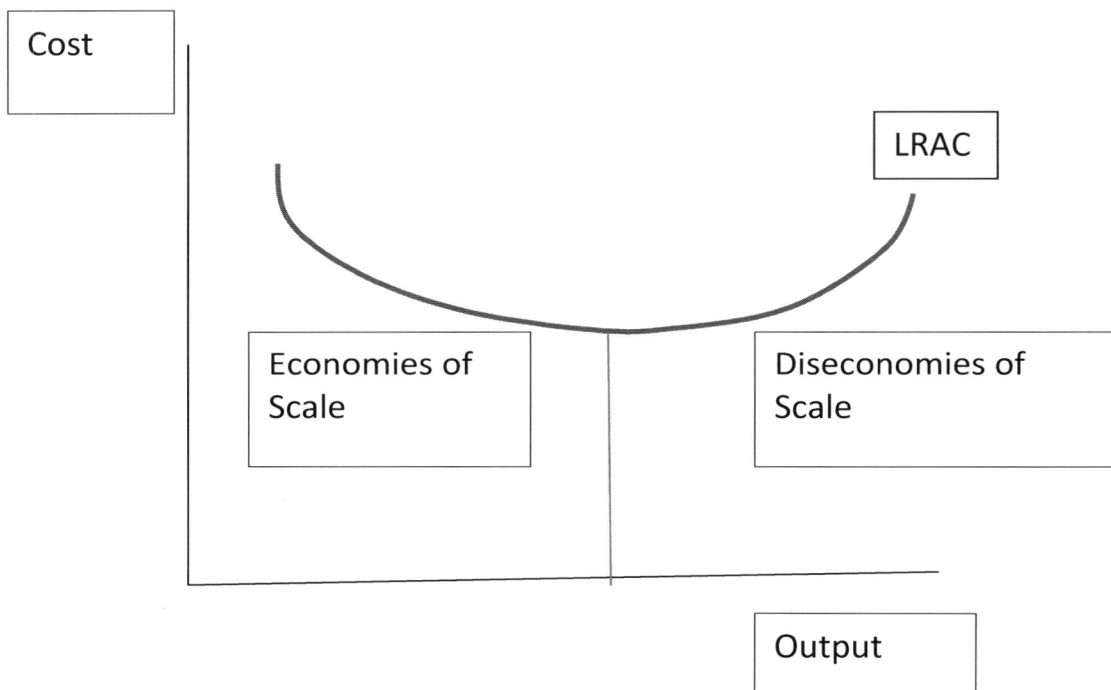

# Economies of Scale

Economies of scale only occur in the long run and are the advantages of large scale production that result in lower unit (average) costs.

Internal Economies of Scale – advantages that arise as a result of the growth of a business:

- ➢ Technical – better and more expensive machinery is available.

- ➢ Managerial – higher skilled staff can be employed.

- ➢ Financial – loans are available with lower interest rates.

- ➢ Purchasing – larger businesses often receive a discount because they are buying in bulk.

- ➢ Risk bearing – spreading risk by having different products or locating in more geographic areas.

External Economies of Scale – advantages businesses gain as a result of the growth of an industry – normally linked to a particular location.

- ➢ Local knowledge and skilled labour

- ➢ Training facilities

- ➢ Good transport links

# Diseconomies of Scale

Diseconomies of scale occur in the long run and are the disadvantages of large scale production that result in higher unit (average) costs.

➢ Poor communication - managing large numbers of staff becomes a challenge which slows down communication.

➢ Reduced motivation - Staff can feel remote and unappreciated so work rate begins to fall and unit costs begin to rise.

# Summary of short and long run cost curves

The short run average cost curve falls due to increasing average returns to the fixed factor of production and rises due to diminishing average returns to the fixed factor of production.

The short run average cost curve forms a U shape curve.

The short run marginal cost curve falls due to increasing marginal returns to the variable factor of production and rises due to diminishing marginal returns to the variable factor of production.

The short run marginal cost curve forms a J shape curve.

The long run average cost curve falls due to economies of scale rises due to diseconomies of scale. The long run average cost curve is made up of a number of short run average cost curves.

# MARKET/INDUSTRY STRUCTURES

## Types of Market Structure

> ➤ Perfect Competition (perfect market).

> ➤ Monopolistic competition – where there a large number of small businesses in the market e.g. electricians, lawyers, hairdressers.

> ➤ Oligopoly – where there is a small number of large businesses who dominate the market e.g. supermarkets, banks, energy suppliers.

> ➤ Duopoly – where only two businesses dominate the market e.g. aircraft manufacturers Airbus and Boeing.

> ➤ Monopoly – can be either a pure monopoly where only one business in the industry or an actual monopoly where one business has greater than 25% of a share in the market.

For this course only knowledge of perfect competition and monopoly needed.

## Determinants of market structure

When deciding which market structure exists the following factors are considered:

> ➤ Number of businesses in the industry.

> ➤ Level of barriers to entry.

> ➤ Nature of the product – how similar or different it is when compared to competitors.

> ➤ Ability of a business to control or influence the price.

> ➤ Definition of the market/industry – what is the market being assessed – is it in a town, a region or across the entire country or continent.

# Monopoly – Characteristics

➢ High barriers to entry.

➢ No competitors.

➢ Only one business.

➢ One unique product.

# Perfect Competition – Characteristics

➢ No barriers to entry.

➢ Large number of buyers and sellers.

➢ No individual business can influence they price.

➢ Al businesses sell an identical product.

➢ Demand for each firm's goods is perfectly elastic.

# Barriers to entry

These prevent any potential competitors from entering an industry and the more of these that exist the closer to a monopoly market structure.

- ➢ Marketing barriers – high spending already done on marketing can have created a brand image and loyally which new firms will find hard to overcome.

- ➢ Legal barriers – certain laws, patents or copyrights can prevent new entrants from entering an industry.

- ➢ Restrictive Trade Practice - ways that existing businesses can try and restrict competition through refusing to buy from a supplier who sells to a rival or setting prices below cost to remove competition (also known as destroyer pricing).

- ➢ Entry Costs - costs to set up in some industries would be very high for new businesses – e.g. aircraft manufacturing.

- ➢ Sunk costs - linked to entry costs but specifically these are costs that could not be recovered if a business fails and includes research and development and advertising.

# Scarcity and Shortage

Scarcity is the basic economic problem and has been discussed fully in previous pages. Scarcity arises because there are limited resources trying to meet unlimited want, causing choices to be made about what, how and for whom to produce.

When any choice is made there is an opportunity cost as an alternative to the choice that is made is sacrificed. There are not enough resources (land, labour, capital) and some resources we have are immobile – they cannot be moved.

> ➢ Occupational immobility – workers are unable to move between jobs because of a lack of skills.

> ➢ Geographical immobility – land cannot be moved as it is hard to make workers move far away for jobs.

A shortage is a temporary situation, whereas scarcity is permanent.

A shortage occurs when demand from consumers is more than supply from businesses for a product.

Scarcity can never be removed but to remove a shortage, prices can be increased to discourage customers or more products made by business.

# LABOUR PRODUCTIVITY

- ➢ Labour Productivity is output per person in a given time period and is found by dividing total output (Q) by the number of workers (L).

- ➢ Labour Productivity = Q/L can be shown as output per worker or output per hour worked.

- ➢ Supply side policies are used to help increase productivity.

- ➢ Productivity is an indicator (measure) of efficiency.

- ➢ Example: if 50 workers produce 10,000 items a day then daily productivity = 10,000/50 = 200 items.

## Factors affecting Productivity

- ➢ Skills and qualifications of workers.

- ➢ Morale of workers.

- ➢ Technological progress.

- ➢ Rules and regulations regarding workers.

# Importance of Labour Productivity

- ➤ Helps economic growth as it allows firms to produce more for lower costs.

- ➤ Rising productivity keeps costs low.

- ➤ If workers become more productive firms can afford to give wage increases.

- ➤ Help to boost exports as can keep prices down through lower costs.

# Why can productivity fall?

- ➤ Strikes and other industrial action.

- ➤ High unemployment.

- ➤ Lack of skills and training amongst workers.

- ➤ Cheaper wages can cause businesses to employ more staff rather than use capital.

# ACTIVITIES

## Research Task 1 - Economic and Free goods

Create two posters: one with images of Economic Goods and one with images of Free Goods.

Provide a short definition of each term on the poster.

## Research Task 2 - Public, Merit and Demerit Goods

Research and then create 3 posters showing examples and a description of:

Public goods, Merit goods, Demerit goods

## Research Task 3 - Positive and Negative Externalities

Research and then create 2 posters showing examples and a description of:

Negative Externalities, Positive Externalities

## Research Task 4 - Competition and Markets Authority

Use the BBC news website and search on Competition and Markets Authority (CMA).

Summarise two recent stories where the CMA has been involved in ensuring competition is taking place.

## Research Task 5 - Production Possibility Curves

Research the ways in which the following governments have tried to increase/improve the birth rate: Romania in the 1960s, Russia, South Korea, France.

## Research Task 6 - Veblen, Giffen and Speculative goods

Research and then create 3 posters showing examples and a description of the following: Veblen Goods, Giffen Goods, Speculative Goods.

## Research Task 7 - Complementary and Substitute goods

Research and create 2 posters showing some examples and a description of the following: Complementary Goods, Substitute Goods.

## Research Task 8 - Elasticity

Research and then create a poster (s) with some examples of goods and services that are price inelastic and some goods and services which are price elastic.

## Research Task 9 - Supply

Using the BBC website or google news and search terms 'poor harvest' and 'bumper harvest' find a recent story for each which has affected the supply and the price of these products.

## Research Task 10 - Shortages and Surpluses

Using google news or BBC websites and search terms 'demand outstrips supply' and 'supply outstrips demand' find recent news stories on products where shortages and surpluses have occurred and the reasons why.

## Research Task 11 - Market Structures

Using the BBC news site, search the terms duopoly, oligopoly and monopoly.

Summarise a news story which features each term and include the country and business (es) involved, the industry they are in and briefly what the article is about.

# Revision Questions Set 1

1. State the basic economic problem. (1)

2. Name the 3 types of economic system. (3)

3. Give the 3 basic economic questions. (3)

4. Identify the limited resources. (3)

5. Define opportunity cost. (1)

6. Give 2 examples of a public good. (2)

7. Give 2 examples of a merit good. (2)

8. Give an example of a negative externality. (1)

9. Define market failure. (1)

10. Name two economic concepts that can be shown on a Production Possibility Curve (PPC). (2)

11. State the number of curves required to show economic growth when drawing a PPC. (1)

# Revision Questions Set 2

1. State 3 factors that may cause the demand curve to shift. (3)

2. Give the formula for calculating Price elasticity of demand. (1)

3. Suggest 3 factors that determine Price elasticity of demand. (3)

4. Draw a fully labelled inelastic demand curve. (3)

5. Draw a fully labelled supply and demand diagram showing clearly the equilibrium price and quantity. (3)

6. On the same diagram drawn for question 5 show the impact of a decrease in the price of a substitute good and a decrease in the costs of production. (3)

# Revision Questions Set 3

1.      State the formula for calculating Total Costs. (1)

2.      Give an example of a Fixed Cost. (1)

3.      Describe a variable cost. (1)

4.      Give the formula for calculating Average Total Cost. (1)

5.      Describe the shape of the Average Total Cost curve. (2)

6.      Describe Marginal Cost. (2)

7.      Describe the difference between the Short Run and the Long Run. (2)

8.      Define Economies and Diseconomies of Scale. (2)

# Demand, Supply and Markets Task

For each scenario state the effect on demand and/or supply.

1      A fall in the price of a complimentary good.

2      An increase in the cost of raw materials.

3      A rise in the price of a substitute good and the removal of a government subsidy.

4      Tastes shifting away from a product and a poor harvest.

5      An increase in electricity costs and a rise in the price of a complimentary good.

6      A tax cut for businesses and an increase in economic growth.

7      A fall in the price of a substitute good and a bumper harvest.

8      Higher wage costs and a rise in people's income.

# EXAM STYLE QUESTIONS

1.   Draw a diagram to show the shape of a short run average cost curve. (2)

2.   Explain, using a diagram, economies and diseconomies of scale. (6)

3.   Describe the basic economic problem. (3)

4.   Describe the characteristics of a monopoly market structure. (3)

5.   Explain reasons for the government intervening in a free market economy. (4)

6.   Describe factors that may affect the price elasticity of demand. (4)

# Research Tasks - Suggested Solutions

Examples of Economic Goods – televisions, kettles, furniture, cars.

Examples of Free Goods – sea water, air.

Examples of Public Goods – lighthouses, street lights, armed forces.

Examples of Merit Goods – education, healthcare.

Examples of De-merit goods – alcohol, tobacco, gambling.

Examples of Positive externalities – vaccinations, prescriptions.

Examples of Negative externalities – noise pollution, traffic pollution.

Examples of Veblen Goods – expensive cars, expensive watches.

Examples of Giffen Goods – rice, bread, potatoes.

Examples of Speculative Goods – shares, gold.

Examples of Complimentary Goods – cars and fuel, shoes and shoe polish, printers and ink cartridges, fish and chips, toothpaste and toothbrush.

Examples of Substitute Goods – Burger King and McDonalds, Coca Cola and Pepsi, margarine and butter, tea and coffee.

# Revision Questions Set 1 – Suggested Solutions

1. State the basic economic problem (1) – Scarcity

2. Name the 3 types of economic system. (3) - Command/Planned, Free Market, Mixed.

3. List the limited resources (3) - Land, Labour and Capital.

4. Define opportunity cost. (1) - The cost of the next best alternative which is sacrificed.

5. Give 2 example of a public good. (2) - Street Lighting, Lighthouses, Armed Forces.

6. Give 2 examples of a merit good. (2) - Education, Healthcare.

7. Give an example of a negative externality. (1) - Noise Pollution, Traffic Pollution.

8. Define market failure. (1) - When the private sector fails to provide the quantity and/or quality of resources desired by customers.

9. State two economic concepts that can be shown on a Production Possibility Curve (PPC)? (2) - Opportunity Cost, Economic Efficiency or Economic Growth.

10. Suggest two other names for a Production Possibility curve. (2) Production Possibility Diagram or Production Possibility Frontier.

11. Give the number of curves required to show economic growth when drawing a PPC? (1) – 2.

# Revision Questions Set 2 – Suggested Solutions

1. State 3 factors that may cause the demand curve to shift.(3) - Changes in price of complimentary goods, changes in price of substitute goods, changes in people's income, a successful advertising or other promotional campaigns.

2. Give the formula for calculating Price elasticity of demand? (1) - % change in Quantity Demand divided by % change in Price.

3. Suggest 3 factors that determine Price elasticity of demand? (3) Number of close substitutes for a product, Is the product a necessity?, Is the product a luxury?, Is the product bought regularly (habitually)?, The definition of the product (i.e. fuel or fuel in Tesco ).

4. Draw a fully labelled inelastic demand curve. (3)

5. Draw a fully labelled supply and demand diagram showing clearly the equilibrium price and quantity. (3)

6. On the same diagram drawn for question 5 show the impact of a decrease in the price of a substitute good and a decrease in the costs of production. (3) - Diagram should show decrease in demand and an increase in supply. New supply line to right of original and new demand line to left of original with new equilibrium at a higher price.

# Revision Questions Set 3 – Suggested Solutions

1. State the formula for calculating Total Costs. (1) - Total Costs = Fixed Costs + Variable Costs.

2. Give an example of a Fixed Cost. (1) - Rent, Loan interest.

3. Describe a variable cost. (1) - A variable cost is a cost which changes directly with output.

4. Give the formula for calculating Average Total Cost. (1) - Average total cost is calculated as total cost / output.

5. Describe the shape of the Average Total Cost curve. (2) - The shape of the average cost curve is U shaped – it falls due to increasing average returns and rises due to diminishing average returns.

6. Describe Marginal Cost. (2) - Marginal cost is the additional cost of one more unit of output.

7. Describe the difference between the Short Run and the Long Run. (2) - The short run time period occurs when at least one factor of production (land, labour, capital) stays the same but in the long run time period all factors of production can change meaning no fixed costs.

8. Define Economies and Diseconomies of Scale. (2) - Economies of scale are savings a business makes as it grows in size and the unit cost fall whereas diseconomies of scale occur when the unit cost of producing more output begins to rise and indicates a business has become too large and difficult to control.

# Demand, Supply and Markets Task – Suggested Solutions

For each scenario state the effect on demand and/or supply. Remember each scenario begins with a diagram showing the equilibrium price and quality with one demand and one supply curve (see page)

1       A fall in the price of a complimentary good - MORE DEMAND - new demand curve to the right of the original.

2       An increase in the cost of raw materials - LESS SUPPLY - new supply curve to the left of the original.

3       A rise in the price of a substitute good and the removal of a government subsidy - MORE DEMAND AND LESS SUPPLY - new demand curve to right of the original and new supply curve to the left of the original.

4       Tastes shifting away from a product and a poor harvest - LESS DEMAND AND LESS SUPPLY - new demand curve to left of the original and new supply curve to the left of the original.

5       An increase in electricity costs and a rise in the price of a complimentary good - LESS SUPPLY AND LESS DEMAND - new supply curve to left of the original and new demand curve to left of the original.

6       A tax cut for businesses and an increase in economic growth - MORE SUPPLY AND MORE DEMAND - new supply curve to the right of the original and a new demand curve to the right of the original.

7       A fall in the price of a substitute good and a bumper harvest - LESS DEMAND AND MORE SUPPLY - new demand curve to left of the original and a new supply curve to the right of the original.

8       Higher wage costs and a rise in people's income - LESS SUPPLY AND MORE DEMAND - new supply curve to the left of the original and a new demand curve to the right of the original.

# Exam Style Questions – Suggested Solutions

1. Draw a diagram to show the shape of a short run average cost curve. (2)

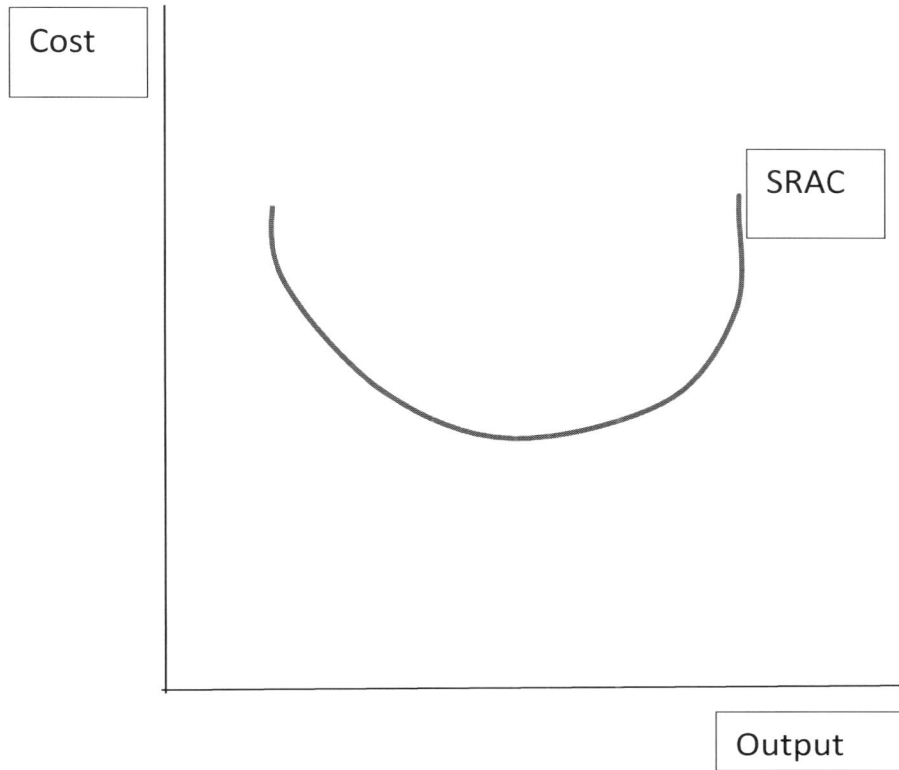

Cost

SRAC

Output

2.    Explain, using a diagram, economies and diseconomies of scale. (6)

The long run is the time period when all factors of production (land, labour, capital) are variable so there are no fixed costs. (1)

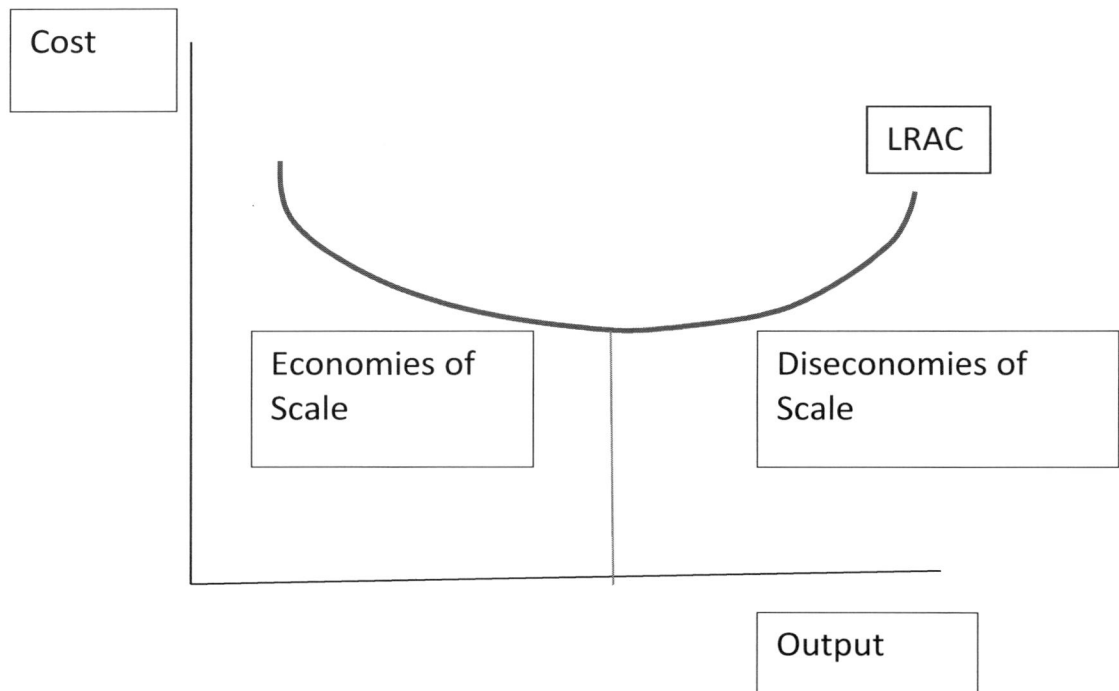

| Cost |
|------|

| LRAC |
|------|

| Economies of Scale | Diseconomies of Scale |
|---|---|

| Output |
|--------|

Economies of scale only occur in the long run and are the advantages of large scale production that result in lower unit (average) costs. (1)

Technical – better and more expensive machinery is available. (1)

Managerial – higher skilled staff can be employed. (1)

Financial – loans are available with lower interest rates which lowers costs. (1)

Purchasing – larger businesses often receive a discount because they are buying in bulk which reduces average costs. (1)

Risk bearing – spreading risk by having different products or locating in more geographic areas. (1)

Diseconomies of scale occur in the long run and are the disadvantages of large scale production that result in higher unit (average) costs. (1)

Poor communication - managing large numbers of staff becomes a challenge which slows down communication and causes unit costs to increase. (1)

Reduced motivation - Staff can feel remote and unappreciated so work rate begins to fall and unit costs begin to rise. (1)

3. Describe the basic economic problem. (3)

The basic economic problem is scarcity (1).

Economic resources of land, labour and capital are used to make goods and provide services that people want and need. (1) However, these resources (land, labour and capital) are scarce (limited) (1) and individuals' wants and needs are unlimited due to greed and technical advances. (1)

4.    Describe the characteristics of a monopoly market structure. (3)

Characteristics of a monopoly structure include:

High barriers to entry. (1)

No competitors. (1)

Only one business in the industry. (1)

Product sold by business is unique. (1)

5.    Explain reasons for the government intervening in a free market
      economy. (4)

Reasons for government intervening in a market include:

Public goods are goods and services that would not be provided in a free
market by the workings of the price mechanism because
businesses/entrepreneurs would not be able to charge for them (1) because
they are:

Non-excludable – once the goods are provided it is not possible to exclude
people from using them even if they have not paid. (1).

This allows free riders to consume goods without paying any money for them.
(1)

Non-rival – this means that the consumption of the good by one person
doesn't diminish the amount available for the next person. (1)

Public goods include street lighting and the armed forces. (1)

Merit goods are goods and services which are considered desirable for all in a country to receive but in a free market not all people would be able to afford them if asked to pay and would therefore not consume or purchase them. (1)

Merit goods would exist in a free market economy and are available in a mixed economy by private sector businesses but only to those who choose to pay. (1)

Merit goods include health care and education. (1)

Demerit goods are goods and services which are considered harmful to society. (1) These goods and services are very profitable to entrepreneurs/businesses and would be over consumed in a free market economy without a government to monitor their use. (1)

Examples of demerit good include alcohol and drugs. (1)

A negative externality occurs when everyone in society faces additional costs over and above those incurred by a business who would not consider these costs when setting their price. (1). An example of a negative externality is noise pollution. (1)

A positive externality occurs when consumers that do not actually purchase a product receive some benefit. (1). An example of a positive externality is prescription medicines. (1)

6.     Describe factors that may affect the price elasticity of demand. (4)

Factors which may affect price elasticity of demand include:

The number of substitutes for a good or service – the more substitutes the more elastic the demand as even a small change in price will cause many customers to buy an alternative product and demand will fall significantly. (1)

The degree of necessity – products that are seen as necessary or are addictive items tend to have inelastic demand and continue to be purchased by most consumers even if price rises significantly. (1)

Luxuries – luxuries will tend to be more elastic in demand following a price change as they are more easily given up by people if they become more expensive. (1)

Goods which are subject to habitual (regular) consumption tend to be more inelastic as less likely to notice the price changes e.g. loaf of bread. (1)

Breadth of definition of a good or service – if a good is broadly defined e.g. fuel then the demand for fuel is fairly inelastic due to it being a necessity (1) but specific brands like fuel from ASDA or fuel from ESSO are likely to be more elastic given the large number of substitutes. (1)

# UNIT TWO – UK ECONOMIC ACTIVITY

## (MACRO) ECONOMIC AIMS/OBJECTIVES

The main aims/objectives of any economy, including the UK, are the following:

➢ Low unemployment/high employment/full employment

➢ Low inflation

➢ Sustained/steady economic growth as measured by GDP (Gross Domestic Product)

➢ Stable Balance of Trade (exports and imports)

We will look at the first 3 aims/objectives in this guide with Balance of Trade a topic for the Global Economic Activity guide.

To achieve these objectives various policies can be used.

# Monetary Policy

Monetary policies are policies that make changes to the base interest rate and the money supply to help achieve the economic objectives.

An Interest Rate is defined as the cost of borrowing and the reward for saving money, given as a percentage.

The base interest rate is set by the Monetary Policy Committee (MPC) of the Bank of England. All other interest rates for loans, mortgages and credit cards are then based on this.

The MPC is a group of 9 people chaired by the Governor of the Bank of England who meet 8 times a year and are tasked with keeping inflation to a target of 2% each month. It is allowed to be 1% above or 1% below the target before the MPC have to officially explain this to government.

# Fiscal Policy

Fiscal policies are policies that make changes to rates of Taxation and Government Spending in order to achieve the economic objectives.

# Supply Side Policy

Supply side policies are policies which aim to achieve the economic objectives by improving the productivity and skills of the people and businesses of a country.

# UNEMPLOYMENT

## Ways to measure unemployment

### Claimant Count

The Claimant Count is published each month and counts the number of people able to claim Job Seekers Allowance (JSA) and/or Universal Credit principally for the reason of being unemployed.

### Labour Force Survey (LFS)

The LFS interviews a sample of approximately 60,000 people each month and counts as unemployed those who currently do not have a job and who:

Were available to start work in the next two weeks, and had actively sought work in the last four weeks or had found a job and were waiting to start.

The numbers from LFS are higher than the claimant count but seen as more accurate and is a similar method to those in other countries which makes comparisons easier.

Not all people of working age are counted as some are classed as economically inactive. These are people who are not in work, but who do not satisfy all the criteria for Labour Force Survey unemployment e.g. parents who are looking after children and are not therefore seeking a job.

# Effects of Unemployment

## Individuals

➢ Reduced income and standard of living for those without a job.

➢ Reduced efficiency as the unemployed worker loses skills, fitness and motivation.

➢ Reduced status – could lead to social exclusion from friends.

➢ Increased physical and mental health problems e.g. stress, reduced quality of diet.

## Businesses

## Negative

➢ As unemployed people will have less income there is a fall in demand for products leading lower sales and profits.

➢ Suppliers also lose customers and suffer falls in sales and profits.

## Positive

➢ More job applicants to choose from when jobs are advertised.

➢ Not as much pressure to pay higher wages to attract staff.

➢ Less risk of industrial action, e.g. strikes, as employees are worried about losing their jobs as they are more easily replaced.

## Government

➢ Reduced taxation revenue for the government as less income tax being received.

➢ Increased burden on taxpayers as they need to fund training for unemployed people and higher benefit payments.

➢ Increases in crime levels and the costs of policing.

➢ Increased burden on the NHS to deal with health issues linked to unemployment.

➢ If unemployment reaches very high levels, then civil unrest like protests and demonstrations can occur.

# Types/Causes of Unemployment

## Cyclical

Cyclical unemployment is associated with a recession/falling economic growth.

Aggregate (overall or total) demand falls for all products so businesses reduce staff and there are no longer enough jobs for those seeking them.

## Structural

Structural unemployment is caused by a mismatch between the skills that workers in the economy can offer, and the skills demanded of workers by employers (also known as the skills gap).

Usually linked to the closure of entire industries e.g. coal mining, shipbuilding where workers are unable to transfer to another business in the industry when the business they work for closes.

## Frictional

Frictional unemployment occurs when people are switching between jobs, either because they have been made redundant or are looking for new employment.

Can also be linked to a lack of knowledge about job vacancies.

## Seasonal

Seasonal unemployment happens in industries such as agriculture, tourism and building where the number of people employed changes depending on the time of year.

# Policies to reduce unemployment

## Fiscal policies to reduce unemployment

### Cutting taxes

When taxes on consumers (e.g. income tax) are reduced this should increase disposable income, which increases demand for products, helping growth and leading to more workers being employed.

When taxes on businesses (e.g. corporation tax) are reduced this allows them to keep more of their profits which they can invest into expanding and creating more jobs.

### Increasing government spending

When government spending is increased this should create jobs in the public sector e.g. more teachers, police officers etc. and give existing government workers more income.

This increases demand for products, helping growth and leading to more workers being employed.

# Monetary policies to reduce unemployment

### Reduce interest rates

When interest rates are lowered this makes it cheaper to borrow money, which encourages spending by consumers. This increases demand for products, creates growth and jobs and therefore reduces unemployment.

When interest rates are lowered it also makes it cheaper for businesses to borrow money which they can use to grow, for example, by opening more shops. This requires more staff which will reduce unemployment.

# Supply side policies to reduce unemployment

Supply side policies are policies aimed at improving aggregate (total) supply by improving the skills of the population and can done in the following ways:

➢ Provide high quality education and training – give workers new skills to find jobs and help occupational immobility. Occupational immobility occurs when people lack the skills to do a range of different jobs.

➢ Give employment subsidies – give businesses financial incentives to employ those people who are long term unemployed.

➢ Have a stricter benefits system – make it less financially worthwhile for people to claim benefits than gaining a job.

➢ Improve geographical immobility to encourage workers to move to different locations to gain employment.

## Ways to improve geographical mobility

➢ Providing affordable housing.

➢ Giving financial help with relocation costs.

➢ Improving transport infrastructure like roads and railways to make travelling easier and quicker.

➢ Ensuring adequate provision of social services e.g. doctors, schooling

## Full Employment

This is a term often used in the topic of unemployment but with no set definition. It can describe a situation where 2-3% of the working population is unemployed and is sometimes referred to as the natural rate of unemployment.

Full employment can also be defined as when the number out of work matches the number of unfilled job vacancies.

Full employment does not mean everyone has a job as there will always be some frictional unemployment as people switch between jobs and are out of work for short periods of time.

# INFLATION

Inflation is a rise in the general level of prices. This does not mean that all prices rise - some may rise; others fall or stay the same.

## Ways to measure inflation

### Consumer Price Index (CPI)

> ➢ Since 2004 this has been the government's official measure for inflation with a target of 2%.

> ➢ Around 180,000 individual prices of nearly 700 items are gathered each month.

> ➢ These 700 items are updated every year to reflect what consumers are purchasing with some items dropping out of the 'shopping basket' and others being added.

> ➢ Items are weighted so changes in price of those purchased most impact the overall figure more.

> ➢ CPI does not include mortgage payments or other housing costs such as repairs, insurance and council tax.

> ➢ CPI measure is a much closer to the method used by the rest of the EU and allows easier comparison.

## Consumer Price Index including housing costs (CPIH)

CPIH is a measure which does include owner occupier housing costs like council tax and is favoured by the Office of National Statistics who produce the inflation and unemployment figures.

## Retail Price Index (RPI)

Until 2004 RPI was the main measure of inflation with a target of 2.5% for the Bank of England to maintain.

The RPI is similar to CPI with a slightly different range of items used and this measure does include some housing costs.

Although no longer the main measure it is still calculated and used as the figure when deciding how much increases in pensions or train fares should be.

## Nominal and real rates

Nominal – the monetary value before the rate of inflation has been considered.

Real – the monetary value after the rate of inflation has been considered.

The real value is more important and when viewing information you need to know if figures are given in 'nominal' terms or 'real' terms.

## Example

Receiving £20 every Christmas from an aunt is the nominal amount but if inflation is 5% each year then the 'real' value of the £20 reduces. This means less can be bought each year with that same amount of money (the £20).

In nominal terms you would be no worse off if you keep receiving £20 each year but in real terms you would be.

## Example

Pay rises are usually given in nominal terms so if someone receives a 2% pay rise and they were earning £30,000 year they would see an increase in pay to £30,600 a year. However if inflation was 5% during the year that pay rise could also be described as a 3% reduction in real terms.

# Effects/problems of high inflation

- ➤ Reduces the 'real' income of people (see above) – if individuals do not receive a pay rise at the same or above the rate of inflation they can purchase less with the same amount of money and in 'real' terms are worse off.

- ➤ Makes savers worse off when inflation is above the interest rate as it reduces the value of savings.

- ➤ High inflation makes British goods more expensive abroad leading to a fall in exports.

- ➤ When inflation is high, individuals are uncertain what to spend money on and businesses may be less likely to invest as uncertain about future costs.

- ➤ Menu Costs – costs involved in changing price lists e.g. catalogues, brochures.

- ➤ Historically high rates of inflation have usually been followed by recession but low inflation rates result in longer periods of growth.

## Deflation

Deflation is a fall in the general level of prices.

Falling prices occur because of less demand which makes it difficult for businesses to make profit and leads to unemployment.

People are reluctant to spend as deflation means products will be cheaper in the future.

Falling share and house prices reduce people's wealth and confidence in making purchases.

# Types/Causes of inflation

## Cost Push

Cost push inflation occurs when the costs of making a product increase at a faster rate than the number of products made leading to increases in unit costs. Costs of making a product include wages, raw materials, VAT (value added tax), energy (electricity and gas).

Wage push inflation is the name given if increases are specifically because of increases in staff costs.

## Demand Pull

Demand pull inflation occurs when the economy is growing (GDP is increasing) too quickly.

Aggregate (total) demand from all consumers is greater than aggregate (total) supply from all businesses – sometimes referred to as 'too much money chasing too few goods'.

Shortages are created in the economy so businesses have to increase prices in response to excess demand.

## Monetary

Monetary Inflation occurs when the money supply (amount of money in economy) is increasing at a faster rate than output (what businesses produce).

It can be caused by the government printing money (quantitative easing) to fund government spending.

# Policies to reduce inflation

## Fiscal policies to reduce inflation

### Raising taxes

Increasing taxes on individuals will cause a fall in their disposable income as they are paying more to the government and decreases demand for products, lowering demand pull inflation.

The reduced demand may however cause slower growth and unemployment.

### Decreasing government spending

When government spending is decreased through reducing public sector pay this is likely to decrease demand for products and in turn inflation.

## Monetary policies to reduce inflation

### Raising interest rates

When interest rates are increased this makes it more expensive to borrow money, which discourages spending by consumers. This reduced demand for product should reduce demand pull inflation.

When interest rates are raised it also makes it more expensive for businesses to borrow money so they are less likely to expand.

Higher mortgage interest payments will reduce homeowner's disposable income and their ability to spend which also reduce demand pull inflation.

# Supply side policies to reduce inflation

Any measure aimed at improving the productive capacity of the economy and are similar to supply side policies for reducing unemployment.

➢ Improvements in education and training of the population.

➢ Reduce the power of trade unions to take industrial action, which would lead to less being produced.

➢ Make planning permission easier to obtain to encourage businesses to grow.

# ECONOMIC GROWTH AND GDP

Economic Growth is a main indicator of how well an economy is performing and occurs when a country is experiencing an increase in Gross Domestic Product (GDP).

GDP is calculated either by measuring all income earned within a country or by measuring all expenditures within a country.

Official figures for GDP in the UK are announced every quarter/3 months with GDP usually given as a percentage which is the % change from the previous 3 months. However it is important to note that GDP itself is a numeric figure.

GDP should be adjusted for inflation and the real GDP is more important than nominal GDP.

GDP figures indicate the size of a country's economy and can also be calculated on a per capita (or per person) basis to show the richness of an economy.

A contraction/shrinkage occurs when there is a decrease in GDP rate in one quarter. A RECESSION occurs when there is a decrease in GDP rate in two consecutive quarters.

# Gross National Product (GNP)

Gross National Product is a secondary measure of assessing how an economy is performing.

It measures the total value of goods produced and services produced by the citizens and businesses of a country no matter where they are based in the world.

For example, the output of Nissan's car factory in Sunderland would be counted within the UK's GDP calculation but not in the UK's GNP figures as Nissan are a Japanese company.

# Measuring GDP

GDP can be measured by calculating national income, national output or national expenditure.

➢ National output adds up all the values of <u>final</u> goods and services produced by businesses produced by all sectors of the economy; agriculture, manufacturing, energy, construction, the service sector and government.

➢ National income adds up all the incomes received from production – wages, rent, dividends, and profits.

➢ National expenditure adds up all spending on <u>final</u> goods and services purchased by households and by government, investment in machinery and buildings. It also includes the value of exports minus imports.

National Expenditure is the most common method and is split into 5 categories which are:

➢ Consumer Spending (C) – spending by people and households in a country which is the largest category.

➢ Business Investment (I) – spending by businesses on machines and factories.

➢ Government Spending (G) – spending by government on education, transports, NHS. It excludes pensions and benefits as they are counted under consumer spending.

➢ Exports (X) – UK produced goods and services sold abroad.

➢ Imports (M) – spending on foreign goods and services by UK citizens.

The calculation for GDP = C+I+G+(X-M).

## Benefits of growth

- ➢ A country is producing or spending more on goods and services than it did in the previous quarter which increases employment, gives people more money and a better standard of living.

- ➢ More tax revenue for Government

- ➢ Less spending on unemployment benefits.

## Costs of growth

- ➢ Not all the increased spending/income is distributed equally amongst the population creating income inequalities.

- ➢ Pollution and environmental damage may be caused.

- ➢ GDP figures include spending on weapons and prisons which may not be desirable for society and does not consider stress or crime.

- ➢ GDP calculation used to measure growth does not consider how long people work.

- ➢ Growth could be caused by over spending and create large and unaffordable debt.

- ➢ Economic growth can cause inflation due to increased spending and demand.

# Business/Trade cycles

History has shown that for most economies the GDP fluctuates over time known as business or trade cycles and can be represented in diagram form.

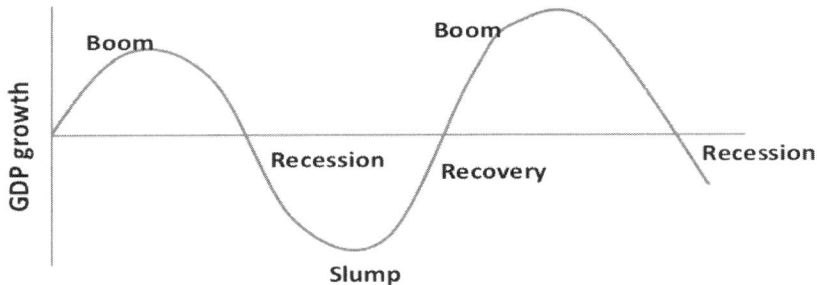

## Stages of the Business/Trade Cycle

> - Boom/Peak – at this stage GDP is increasing. Incomes, employment and tax revenue are high and inflation may start to increase.

> - Recession – at this stage GDP has fallen for 2 consecutive quarters (a six month period). Income, employment and tax revenues are falling whereas benefit payments increase.

> - Slump – at this stage GDP falls for longer than 2 consecutive quarters. Issues similar to a recession but more severe with even higher unemployment, lower demand and less tax revenues.

> - Recovery – this stages follows from either a recession or a slump and GDP begins to increase. Incomes, employment and tax revenues begin to rise again.

# Creating growth – demand side policies

Growth can be created if Consumer spending (C), business investment (I), government spending (G) or Exports (X) are increased or Imports (M) reduced.

## Monetary policies to create growth

Lowering interest rates can encourage more Consumer Spending as lower interest rates make it cheaper to borrow money, reduce mortgage repayments and reduce the incentive to save. This increased spending creates growth.

Lowering interest rates can encourage more Business Investment as lower interest rates make it cheaper to borrow money so businesses are more likely to borrow and grow their business which may create jobs. This increased employment leads to more spending and creates growth.

Lowering interest rates can reduce the exchange rate value of the pound sterling which increases exports (X) as they become cheaper and decreases imports (M) as they become more expensive.

## Fiscal policies to create growth

Reducing taxes for individuals can increase Consumer Spending (C) as it provides more disposable income to spend.

Reducing taxes for businesses can increase Business Investment (I) as it allows them to keep more of their profits.

Increasing Government Spending (G) (discussed later in guide)

# Creating growth - Supply side policies

Economic Growth will happen if a country increases its productive capacity – i.e. if there is an increase in the quantity or quality of its resources (land, labour, capital) allowing more goods and services to be produced.

A Production Possibility Curve is used to show Economic Growth occurring in this way (covered more in Economics of the Market Unit).

Growth can be achieved by:

➢ Increasing investment in new factories, roads, and infrastructure.

➢ Increasing the working population through immigration and higher birth rate.

➢ Better education and training.

# TAXATION – FISCAL POLICIES

Taxes are paid by individuals and businesses within a country to a government who use these to fund spending. Taxes are classified in a number of ways but note that a tax will be either direct or indirect and progressive or regressive.

## Direct taxes

A direct tax is a tax on income and wealth which are taken directly from individuals and firms - income tax, national insurance and corporation tax.

## Indirect taxes

An indirect tax is a tax not directly taken from people but are placed on various products and are avoided by those who do not consume those products – Value Added Tax, Road tax, Duties on betting, alcohol, tobacco, air travel.

The business who pays the tax to the government normally adds the tax to the price, making the product more expensive to the consumer.

## Progressive taxes

A progressive tax takes into account the ability of people to pay. Those with more income pay more so the richer pay more than the poor.

A progressive tax will take a larger percentage/proportion of income as income rises. Examples include income tax.

## Regressive taxes

Regressive taxes take no account of the ability of people to pay and are normally at a flat rate for everyone.

This means that it hits lower income individuals harder as they pay proportionately more. Examples include Value Added Tax and duties on alcohol and tobacco (cigarettes).

# Fiscal Policies to reduce income inequality

## Taxation

- Increase rates of income tax – as it is a progressive tax then high earners will pay more and revenue can be redistributed by government.

- Reduce VAT – as it is a regressive tax then lower earners could pay less of their income.

- Increase rates of inheritance or capital gains tax which is usually paid by the richest in society which can then be redistributed.

## Spending

- Increase spending on infrastructure e.g. Crossrail or High Speed 2 to create jobs.

- Increase benefit payments to increase income of those who are unemployed.

- Increase the pay of public sector workers.

# GOVERNMENT SPENDING - FISCAL POLICIES

Government spending covers all spending by central government, local government and public corporations.

## Types of Spending

- Capital spending – spending on building of hospitals, schools, roads.

- Current Spending – the running costs of government mainly wages/salaries of public sector workers.

- Transfer payments – a payment to individuals or firms for which there is no benefit given in return e.g. unemployment benefit, child benefit and pensions.

When government spending is greater than taxation then money must be borrowed.

This money is borrowed from individuals, banks, insurance companies and pensions funds both within a country and abroad and the governments of other countries.

The borrowing required by the government each year is called the Public Sector Net Cash Requirement (PSNCR).

PSNCR is measured in £ billion and as a percentage of GDP.

When the government spends more than its revenue from tax it is called a BUDGET DEFICIT. When the government brings in more tax than it spends it is called a BUDGET SURPLUS.

## National Debt

- National Debt is the total amount that the public sector owes to those who have loaned it money.

- When there is a budget deficit then national debt will increase.

- When there is a budget surplus then there may be a reduction in national debt.

## Reducing the Deficit or Reducing the Debt

- If you read or hear that the deficit has been reduced this still means that spending is more than income but less than it has been.

- Reducing the deficit still therefore adds to the National Debt.

- Reducing the debt can only happen if there is a budget surplus (spending is less than income) has occurred during a year.

## Austerity

- Austerity means the measures taken by a government to reduce a budget deficit/create a budget surplus.

## Ways to reduce a Budget Deficit

- Reducing government spending – e.g. by cutting benefits or public sector jobs.

- Increasing rates of direct or indirect taxation to increase tax revenue.

- Widen range of goods and services taxed.

- Selling government owned assets

- Increase or begin charging for government services e.g. hospital car parks.

## Effects of having a Budget Deficit

➤ Government will have to borrow money.

➤ National debt will increase.

➤ Debt interest repayments are increased leaving less money for other areas of spending.

➤ Crowding out – high government borrowing may mean there is less money available to lend to the private sector.

➤ Inflation – monetary policy suggests that if PSNCR is financed by borrowing from banks, this could increase the money supply and lead to inflation.

## Problems reducing the National Debt

➤ Reducing the debt may involve less government spending which could increase unemployment as fewer public sector jobs.

➤ Reducing the debt may require increases in rates of indirect taxation like VAT resulting in increased income inequality as these taxes are regressive (see above for more information on regressive taxes).

➤ Reducing the debt may involve increases in rates of direct taxation like income tax which lowers disposable income and may result in less spending and less economic growth.

➤ All these problems are also likely when trying to reduce a budget deficit.

# CIRCULAR FLOW OF INCOME

The circular flow of income is a way of showing how money flows/moves in an economy and can be shown using a diagram.

Diagrams can be created showing a two, three or four sector economy and displayed in a number of ways. The one below shows a four sector economy.

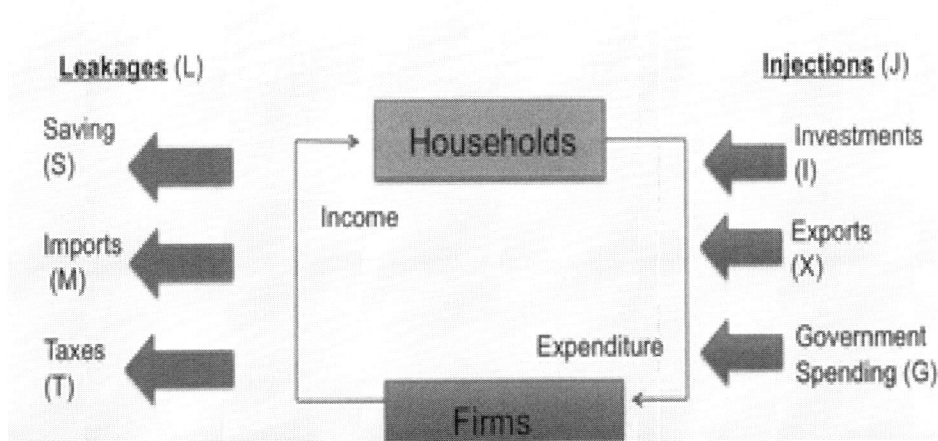

A two sector economy would have households and firms/businesses only.

Households would own the resources (land, labour, capital) which they provide to firms/businesses.

In return businesses give households income, such as rent, wages, interest and profits which they then spend again (consumer spending) and the income/money continues to flow between them.

A three sector economy would have households, businesses and government.

A four sector economy is closest to the real world and includes trade with other countries and a number of leakages/withdrawals and injections.

## Injections

Injections to the circular flow of income increase GDP and are any spending that is not consumer spending.

Three types of injections exist:

> - Investment (I) - spending by businesses. This is normally on capital goods, e.g. machinery.

> - Exports – (X) - money spent by overseas firms and individuals on British goods.

> - Government Spending – (G) spending in the economy of the public sector.

## Leakages

This is any withdrawal of money from the circular flow of income and reduces the value of the economy (GDP).

There are 3 types of leakages:

> - Savings – (S) - money that consumers save from their income.

> - Imports – (M) - amount spent by UK firms and individuals on foreign goods and services.

> - Taxation – (T) - the amount of revenue collected by government.

## National income equilibrium

The circular flow diagram is a way to show national income.

When Injections and Leakages are the same then national income equilibrium exists.

If leakages are more than injections then national income falls.

If injections are more than leakages national income rises and there is economic growth.

## Examples

Exports decrease – this causes a decrease in an injection and therefore a reduction in national income.

Interest rates increase – this encourages more saving (S) which will increase a leakage and reduce national income.

Income tax decreases – this reduces taxation (T) which will decrease a leakage and increase national income.

# The Multiplier

The multiplier describes the situation where a change in an injection or leakage in the circular flow causes a greater overall change in the value of the economy.

> ➢ If an injection increases or a leakage decreases, it will be a positive multiplier effect.

> ➢ If a leakage increases or injection decreases, it will be a negative multiplier effect.

The size of the multiplier is dependent on the % of income that is spent (consumed) and the % of income that is saved.

> ➢ Marginal Propensity to Consume (MPC) measures how much of extra income is spent.

> ➢ Marginal Propensity to Save (MPS) measures how much of extra income is saved.

Formula for the Multiplier = 1/MPS or 1/1-MPC

If the MPS is 0.1 then the multiplier would be 10. This means that national income would increase by ten times the amount of the increase in investment.

## Example

The government increases spending and gives doctors a £1000 pay rise. If every doctor saves 10% of the extra income the MPS is 0.1 and they will save £100 and MPC is 0.9 they spend £900.

The £900 of consumer spending becomes £900 of income to other households. Assuming MPC and MPS continue to be the same then £90 is saved and £810 is spent.

If the example continues then the increase to national income (the value of the economy) would be £10,000 more than it was before the £1000 investment.

## Importance of the multiplier

An increase in any injection into the circular flow of income will increase national income by more than the increase in injection.

A decrease in any injection will decrease national income by more than the initial decrease.

Allows government to know how much they need to spend in order to improve the overall economy e.g. if they wish £10 billion more into the economy and they know the multiplier is 5 then they should increase spending by £2 billion.

# NATIONAL INCOME (NI)

## Uses of national income statistics

- Measure economic growth and changes in standards of living.

- Help government decision making by assessing the state of the economy.

- Compare economic growth and standard of living data between countries.

- Identify countries that are in need of aid – those with low National Income.

- Calculate contributions that countries should make to international organisations such as the World Bank and EU.

## Difficulties measuring national income statistics

- Errors and omissions – data not collected or calculated incorrectly.

- Shadow/hidden economy – people don't show what they earn or produce – to escape paying tax or continue to claim benefits.

- Under-recording of output - some goods and services not included because money doesn't change hands e.g. housework, DIY

- Figures must take into account inflation so real increases or decreases can be measured.

# Difficulties comparing national income statistics

➢ Methods of calculating national income may differ over time or between countries.

➢ Standard of living is measured by income per head so population figures also need to be correct.

➢ Figures do not show differences in working conditions or hours worked between countries.

➢ No differences in income distribution or equality across a population are shown in the national income figure.

➢ Social costs such as pollution are not taken into account.

➢ Spending on defence or prisons may increase national income but does not benefit the standard of living of people and are not desired by many.

# SCOTTISH ECONOMY

Since the creation of the Scottish parliament a number of decisions are now 'devolved' from the UK parliament in Westminster to be made by the parliament in Edinburgh.

Devolved powers include those over:

> agriculture, forestry and fisheries, education and training, environment, health and social services – e.g. no prescription charges.

> housing, law and order, local government, sport and the arts, tourism and some aspects of transport – e.g. no forth road bridge toll.

## In 2012 the Scotland Act gave more powers

> a new Scottish rate of income tax to be in place from April 2016.

> new borrowing powers for the Scottish Government.

> full control of stamp duty land tax and landfill tax from April 2015.

> the power to introduce new taxes, subject to agreement of the UK Government.

> giving Scottish Ministers powers relating to the misuse of drugs, the drink-drive limit, the national speed limit and the administration of elections to the Scottish Parliament.

## Scotland's budget deficit may be different from the UK as a whole due to

- Scottish government having devolved powers to adjust some benefits.

- Scottish government having devolved powers to set Income Tax bands and rates.

- Spending on infrastructure projects like the new Forth Crossing or Edinburgh trams.

- Free prescriptions

- Free university fees

- Free elderly homecare

- No air passenger duty for under 16s

## Effects if Scotland increased income tax

### Positives

> Extra tax revenue from income tax receipts.

> Increased income tax receipts may be spent on benefits/social services/communities. This could result in a better standard of living for some.

> Increasing income tax could lead to a more even distribution of income in Scotland.

> Increasing income tax could lead to lower inflation due to the decrease in demand.

> ### Negatives

> Consumers have less disposable income to spend.

> Lower demand in Scotland and less income/profit for businesses.

> Less profit for businesses could result in business closures which could lead to higher unemployment.

> Business closures/higher unemployment could lead to lower economic growth.

If income tax was reduced in Scotland, compared to other parts of the UK, then the above points would be reversed with the negatives becoming positives and vice versa.

# RESEARCH TASKS

## Research Task 1 - Deflation

Research the deflation that each of the countries below experienced, when it happened, how long it lasted and its impact:

Japan, Republic of Ireland, United States, Hong Kong

## Research Task 2 - Hyperinflation

When inflation is rising rapidly this is known as HYPERINFLATION

Research the hyperinflation that each of the countries below experienced, when it happened and its impact:

Hungary, Zimbabwe, Germany

## Research Task 3 - GDP and economic growth

Use www.countryeconomy.com

Prepare a report comparing two countries – one should be a European country and one an African country.

Include definitions and information about GDP, GDP per capita, life expectancy, population and Human Development index rating.

# Research Task 4 – Business Cycle

Research how many times there has been a recession in the following countries since 1970.

UK, France, Portugal, Japan

For each country find out how long each recession/slump lasted and the longest time period from one to another

# Research Task 5 – Direct and Indirect Tax

Choose one UK direct tax and one UK indirect tax to research.

Find out when it was first introduced in the UK, who pays this tax, what the current rate or rates are and how much money it brings in for the UK government.

# Research Task 6 – Canons of Taxation

Research Adam Smith's 4 canons of taxation – equity, economy, certainty and convenience - and include a description of each canon. Note that canons of taxation will not be asked about specifically in an exam question but this is for further knowledge of taxation.

# Research Task 7 – Circular Flow of Income

Using Google images, create a poster with 4 different examples of a circular flow of income diagram.

# REVISION TASKS

## Revision Questions Set 1

1.  Give 3 (macro) economic objectives. (3)
2.  State 2 ways of measuring unemployment. (2)
3.  Name 3 types/causes of unemployment. (3)
4.  Give the name of the main measure of inflation. (1)
5.  Give the name of another measure of inflation. (1)
6.  Identify what the initials GDP stand for. (1)
7.  Give the full meaning of the abbreviation GNP (1)
8.  Describe the difference between GDP and GNP. (2)
9.  Name any 4 components of GDP/National Income when using the expenditure method. (4)
10. Describe the difference between Monetary and Fiscal Policy. (2)

## Revision Questions Set 2

1.  Give the full name for PSNCR. (1)
2.  Suggest the difference between a budget deficit and the national debt. (2)
3.  Give the full name for MPC and MPS. (2)
4.  Suggest the formula for the Multiplier. (2)
5.  Give 2 benefits of Economic Growth. (2)
6.  Give 2 costs of Economic Growth. (2)
7.  Give 2 uses of National Income Statistics (2)
8.  Give 2 problems of measuring National Income. (2)
9.  Name 2 direct and 2 indirect taxes. (4)
10. Define a recession. (1)

# What's the question?

Prepare a suitable economic question to fit the following answers:

1    Structural Unemployment

2    Counts the number of people claiming Job seekers Allowance

3    2%

4    When the general level of prices falls

5    Unemployment caused by a recession

6    Demand Pull inflation

7    Measured by the Gross Domestic Product

8    Reduce interest rates and reduce taxation

9    Provide more education and training and have a stricter benefits system

10    Supply-Side Policies

# EXAM STYLE QUESTIONS

7.    Explain how monetary policy could be used to achieve economic growth. (4)

8.    Explain how fiscal policies could be used to reduce inflation. (4)

9.    Explain how supply side policies could achieve low unemployment. (4)

10.   Describe the difference between nominal and real terms. (2)

11.   Describe the stages of the business/trade cycle. (4)

12.   Describe how the main measure of inflation is calculated. (2)

13.   Describe problems using national income statistics when comparing the economies of different countries. (4)

# REVISION TASKS – SOLUTIONS

## Revision Questions Set 1 – Suggested Solutions

1.  Give 3 (macro) economic objectives (3) - Low inflation, low unemployment, steady economic growth, stable balance of payments.

2.  State 2 ways of measuring unemployment. (2) - Claimant Count and Labour Force Survey.

3.  Name 3 types/causes of unemployment. (3) - Cyclical, Frictional, Structural, Seasonal.

4.  Give the name of the main measure of inflation. (1) - Consumer Price Index.

5.  Give the name of another measure of inflation. (1) - Retail Price Index, CPIH.

6.  Identify what the initials GDP stand for. (1) - Gross Domestic Product.

7.  Give the full meaning of the abbreviation GNP (1) - Gross National Product.

8.  Describe the difference between GDP and GNP. (2) - GDP measures all output within the borders of a country whereas GNP measures all output by the businesses and individuals of a country no matter where in the world this happens.

9.  Name any 4 components of GDP/National Income when using the expenditure method. (4) - Consumer Spending (C) , Business Investment (I), Government Spending (G), Exports (X)  and Imports (M).

10. Describe the difference between Monetary and Fiscal Policy. (2) - Monetary policy involves adjusting interest rates and money supply to achieve economic objectives whereas fiscal policies involve making changes to taxation and government spending.

# Revision Questions Set 2 – Suggested Solutions

1.	Give the full name for PSNCR. (1) - Public Sector Net Cash Requirement.

2.	Describe the difference between a budget deficit and the national debt. (2) – a budget deficit is when government spending is greater than income from taxation over one year whereas national debt is the total amount a nation owes to those who have loaned it money over many years and decades.

3.	Give the full name for MPC and MPS. (1) - Marginal Propensity to Consumer and Marginal Propensity to Save.

4.	Suggest the formula for the Multiplier. (1) - 1/MPS or 1/1-MPC.

5.	Give 2 benefits of Economic Growth. (2) - Increased standard of living, more employment, more tax revenues, less benefit payments.

6.	Give 2 costs of Economic Growth. (2) - does not consider hours worked, resources used up, pollution caused, does not show if income is distributed equally.

7.	Give 2 uses of National Income Statistics (2) - to calculate economic growth, to decide how much to contribute to international organisations like the EU, to assess how well government policies have been.

8.	Give 2 problems of measuring National Income. (2) hidden economy not included, resources available to calculate, methodology may change, figures must take into account inflation.

9.	Name 2 direct and 2 indirect taxes. (4) Direct – income tax, council tax, corporation tax, inheritance tax, national insurance Indirect – VAT, Air Passenger Duty, Road Tax, Excise duties on cigarettes.

10.	Define a recession. (1) – when the Gross Domestic Product (GDP) decreases/falls in two consecutive quarters/six month period resulting in negative growth.

# What's the Question? – Suggested Solutions

1   Describe the type of unemployment linked to a closure of industries - Structural Unemployment.

2   Describe the Claimant Count measure of unemployment - Counts the number of people claiming Job seekers Allowance.

3   Give the current target rate for the Consumer Price Index inflation rate - 2%.

4   Describe deflation - When the general level of prices falls.

5   Describe cyclical unemployment - Unemployment caused by a recession.

6   Which type of inflation is caused by too much demand - Demand Pull inflation.

7   How is economic growth measured? Measured by the Gross Domestic Product.

8   Identify policies to reduce unemployment or create economic growth - Reduce interest rates and reduce taxation.

9   Identify supply side policies to reduce unemployment or create economic growth - Provide more education and training and have a stricter benefits system.

10  Name the policies that aim to increase the productivity and skills of a nation - Supply-Side Policies

# EXAM STYLE QUESTIONS – SOLUTIONS

1. Explain how monetary policy could be used to achieve economic growth.

   (4)

Lower/reduce interest rates is the monetary policy which will help achieve economic growth.

Lower interest rates benefit consumers as they are more likely to borrow money as they will have less to pay back (1). They will then spend this money on goods and services which will lead to an increase in the Consumer Spending component of GDP used to measure growth (1). Consumers are also likely to have more money to spend as mortgage interest payments will fall (1). Lowering interest rates reduces the reward for saving money resulting in consumers being more likely to spend and create growth (1).

The Business Investment component of GDP will increase as businesses are able to borrow money cheaper than before which they will use to invest more in machinery and technology (1).

Further impacts on the export and import components are likely if interest rates are lowered which are discussed in the Global Economic Activity guide.

2. Explain how fiscal policies could be used to reduce inflation. (4)

Increasing tax rates like income tax or value added tax (VAT) would reduce inflation. Higher income tax rates reduce the disposable income of consumers meaning they have less available to spend from their pay (1). This leads to less demand for products and a reduction in demand pull inflation (1).

Higher VAT rates make products more expensive and this leads to a reduction in their demand (1).

Reducing government spending would also reduce inflation. Less money being spent by the government will create less demand for goods and services in an economy resulting in less employment and lower demand for products which will lead to a fall in demand pull inflation (1).

3.    Explain how supply side policies could achieve low unemployment. (4)

Supply side policies aim to improve the productivity of businesses and people in a country and can help reduce unemployment by:

Providing high quality education and training which will give people the necessary skills and qualifications needed to do the jobs that are available (1).

Giving employment subsidies that will allow businesses to employ those people who are long term unemployed (1).

Having a stricter benefits system which makes it less financially rewarding to claim benefits and not work (1).

Improving geographical immobility to encourage workers to move to different locations where jobs exist (1). This immobility can be caused by poor transport links, lack of housing and schooling so policies to improve these areas can help fill available jobs (1 dev).

4.    Describe the difference between nominal and real terms. (2)

Nominal terms is the money value at the current time (1) whereas real terms take into account the rate of inflation (1). Figures given in real terms are considered more important and caution must be used when data is presented until you are clear whether figures are represented in nominal or real terms (1 dev).

5.    Describe the stages of the business/trade cycle. (4)

Boom – GDP, employment and incomes all rising (1). Inflation may begin to rise. Large amounts of tax revenue being received (1 dev).

Recession – GDP falls for two consecutive quarters (1). Employment and incomes fall as less demand (1 dev). Inflation begins to fall (1 dev). Benefit payments increase (1 dev).

Slump – a longer period of time when GDP is falling (1). Similar issues to a recession with more severe falls in employment and tax revenues and higher benefit payments required (1). Inflation not likely to be a concern (1 dev).

Recovery – Follows a slump or recession and GDP beings to rise again (1). Employment and tax revenues rise and benefit payments become lower (1 dev).

6.  Describe how the main measure of inflation is calculated. (2)

The main measure of inflation is the Consumer Price index. This is calculated monthly by the Office for National Statistics (1) and tracks the prices of around 700 different products across 20,000 outlets with 180,000 individual prices being checked (1). The products are updated annually (1) and are weighted so that changes to the price of more frequently purchased items have a bigger impact on the overall figures (1). The current target rate for CPI inflation is 2% (1).

7.  Describe problems using national income statistics when comparing the economies of different countries. (4)

The problems in using national income statistics to compare economies include:

The resources and methods of calculating national income may differ over time or between countries (1).

Standard of living is measured by income per head so population figures need to be correct (1).

Figures do not show differences in working conditions or hours worked between countries (1).

No differences in income distribution or equality across a population are shown in the national income figure (1).

# UNIT THREE – GLOBAL ECONOMIC ACTIVITY

# ABSOLUTE ADVANTAGE

The theory of absolute advantage states that if 2 countries are each more efficient in making a product, then they should focus solely (specialise) in that product and then trade with the other country.

|  | UK | BURUNDI |
|---|---|---|
| CARS | 10 | 5 |
| TV's | 4 | 10 |

The table above shows the amount of cars and TVs that could be produced by 2 countries, UK and Burundi when they split their resources exactly between two products.

If the theory of absolute advantage is applied then in this example the UK should produce only cars resulting in 20 cars being made and Burundi should produce only TV's resulting in 20 TVs being produced.

# COMPARATIVE ADVANTAGE

Comparative Advantage refers to the situation where a country has an absolute advantage in all products.

This theory states that countries should still specialise in the product where they have a comparative advantage i.e. that in which they have the lowest opportunity cost.

World output will rise and living standards in both countries will rise.

|  | UK | BURUNDI |
|---|---|---|
| CARS | 7 | 21 |
| TV's | 5 | 10 |

The table above shows the amount of cars and TVs that could be produced by 2 countries, UK and Burundi when they split their resources exactly between two products.

Applying the theory of comparative advantage to this example Burundi should produce only cars as they are three times better than the UK at producing that product. The UK should produce TV's because the disadvantage (opportunity cost) is not as much.

## Why do countries have an absolute or comparative advantage?

- ➢ Some countries have supplies of certain natural resources e.g. the UK has oil and Japan doesn't.

- ➢ Some countries have climatic advantages e.g. Spain can grow oranges, the UK can't.

- ➢ Some countries have the workers with the skills and knowledge.

# GAINS FROM TRADE/REASONS FOR FREE TRADE/DISADVANTAGES OF TRADE BARRIERS

➢ Free trade offers consumers more variety in the types of goods and services they purchase.

➢ Free trade allows goods to enter a country without trade barriers so the goods are cheaper.

➢ Free trade provides competition to domestic businesses who have to ensure they are efficient and producing high quality goods.

➢ Removes the threat of retaliation from other countries.

➢ Increases the volume of world trade and the level of world output rises.

# BARRIERS TO TRADE/IMPORT RESTRICTIONS/PROTECTIONISM

## Definition

Ways which trade between countries is restricted in some way – normally through measures to reduce the number of imports coming into a country.

> Tariff - A tax or duty on a good coming into a country which increases the price of the good and makes it less competitive.

> Quota - A physical restriction on the number of goods coming into a country.

> Embargo - a complete ban on trade with a particular country or for a particular product.

> Subsidies - these are given by government to domestic businesses to allow them to compete more strongly by making it cheaper for them to produce their product.

> Favouring - government may choose domestic businesses when awarding contracts for public sector projects.

## Advantages of Trade Barriers/Protectionism

> To protect jobs in a country.

> To protect new industries within a country.

> To prevent dumping where products are sold in another country at very low prices.

> For political reasons to show unhappiness with another country.

> For health and safety reasons.

# BALANCE OF PAYMENTS

The Balance of Payments show a country's trading transactions with the rest of the world over a period of time.

The Balance of Payment Account is divided into 2 broad sections with a number of items/components within each section:

## Section 1 - Current Account

The Current Account section shows the money received from abroad (exports) and money spent abroad (imports) and gives an idea of a country's trading (buying and selling) performance.

### Balance of Trade in Goods

Visible Trade is the export and import of manufactured goods.

### Balance of Trade in Services

Invisible Trade is the export and import of services e.g. banking, transport, insurance, tourism.

### Net Investment Income

Interest, profits and dividends received on UK investments overseas less interest, profits and dividends paid to foreigners investing in the UK.

### Transfers

These are normally payments and receipts to and from the UK government and the EU, international organisations and aid (usually a deficit).

# Section 2 - Capital/Financial Account

The Capital Account shows all purchases and sales of assets to and from the UK.

## Foreign Direct Investment (FDI)

Investments in land, premises and equipment by UK companies setting up branches overseas or vice versa.

## Direct Portfolio Investment

Purchases of UK stocks and shares by foreigners and purchase of foreign stocks and shares overseas by UK residents.

## Movements of Income

UK nationals living abroad transferring money into UK banks or vice versa.

## Short Term Capital Flows (hot money)

Investment in UK by foreigners to take advantage of higher UK interest rates than elsewhere in world or vice versa.

# UK International Trade Situation

Overall the UK has a balance of trade deficit – imports of goods and services are higher than the exports of goods and services.

These are the first two items in the current account section of the Balance of Payments.

## UK Trade in Goods

> Usually a deficit as it's now cheaper to produce goods abroad because of lower wages, lower rents and less strict health and safety regulation.

> Improvements in transport e.g. container ships allow products to be made elsewhere.

> Reduction within the UK of natural resources like coal and oil.

> Low investment in manufacturing and poorer reputation for reliability and design.

## UK Trade in Services

> Usually a surplus as banking, insurance and financial services require higher level of education.

> Skills, knowledge, training and expertise in these professions is higher in the UK than elsewhere.

> Helped by tourism and the many tourist attractions in the UK.

# FOREIGN DIRECT INVESTMENT (FDI)

## Benefits of FDI

➢ Increases employment and income – with multiplier effect for an economy.

➢ Exchange of new technology and management techniques.

➢ Increases choice and variety for consumers.

➢ Increased competition could increase efficiency and reduce costs/prices.

## ➢ Disadvantages of FDI

➢ Profits leave country and return to home country.

➢ Reliance on foreign firms who may lack loyalty and leave.

➢ Top jobs may go to foreign employees.

➢ Local businesses could be unable to compete and close.

## Why locate in Scotland?

➢ Good Infrastructure – roads, airports, communications.

➢ Government assistance through regional grants may be available.

➢ A well-educated and skilled labour force.

➢ Quality universities and research facilities.

➢ English speaking – important for US firms.

# Improving Balance of Trade/ Current Account

To improve a balance of trade or current account deficit, imports need to be lowered or exports increased.

> ➤ To reduce imports, trade barriers can be used but other countries could retaliate.

> ➤ Increasing interest rates (monetary policy) can discourage spending in an economy and reduce demand for imports but could impact other components of GDP and lead to unemployment.

> ➤ Supply side policies e.g. improved education and training which increases the productivity and efficiency of the economy can improve competitiveness and help make exports more attractive.

> ➤ Increasing direct taxes (fiscal policy) reduces disposable income to remove demand for imports.

> ➤ Give subsidies to home producers to make them more competitive with imports.

> ➤ A depreciation in the exchange rate could help to boost demand abroad for UK exports because British firms will be able to sell more cheaply.

> ➤ A lower exchange rate should also cause imports into the UK to become relatively more expensive and may reduce their popularity.

# EXCHANGE RATES

An exchange rate is the rate at which one currency trades against another on the foreign exchange market.

## Factors affecting demand and supply for exchange rates

Exchange rates will fall/depreciate if there is a fall in demand or a rise in supply.

Exchange rates will rise/appreciate if there is a rise in demand or a fall in supply.

### Interest Rates

If UK interest rates rise relative to elsewhere, it will become more attractive to deposit money in the UK and demand for sterling will rise leading to hot money inflows.

A lower interest rate causes a fall/depreciation and results in hot money outflows.

### Inflation

If inflation in the UK is lower than elsewhere, then UK exports will become more competitive and there will be an increase in demand for Pound Sterling to buy UK goods.

Foreign goods will be less competitive and so UK citizens will buy less imports.

Countries with lower inflation rates tend to see an appreciation in the value of their currency.

## Speculation

If speculators believe the pound sterling will rise in the future, they will demand more now to be able to make a profit. This increase in demand will cause the value to rise.

## Imports and Exports

An increase in demand for UK goods and services abroad (exports) will increase demand for pound sterling.

An increase in demand for foreign goods and services (imports) will increase the supply of pound sterling.

## Tourism

An increase in people visiting the UK will increase demand for pound sterling.

An increase in people from the UK travelling abroad will increase supply of pound sterling.

# Exchange Rate comparisons

## Weak/Depreciating Currency - £1 = $1 becomes £1 = $0.50

- ➢ Price of Exports (X) falls so more exports.

- ➢ Price of Imports (M) rises so less imports.

- ➢ Higher inflation due to higher import prices.

- ➢ Higher growth due to improved balance of trade.

- ➢ More hot money outflows.

## Strong/Appreciating Currency - £1 = $1 becomes £1 = $2

➤ Price of Exports (X) rises so less exports.

➤ Price of Imports (M) falls so more imports.

➤ Lower inflation due to lower import prices.

➤ Lower growth due to poorer balance of trade.

➤ More hot money inflows.

# EXCHANGE RATE SYSTEMS

## Fixed Exchange Rates

When the exchange rate with another currency always stays the same with the government ensuring this happens.

Between 1949 and 1967 the price of pound sterling was fixed at £1=$2.80

Less demand for the pound would require the government to buy £s using its reserves of foreign currencies.

More demand for the pound would result in the government selling £s and buying foreign currencies.

### Advantages

> Promotes international trade as there is more certainty over the exchange rate.

> Could help to keep inflation stable – no fluctuations in imported raw material prices.

> Currency less vulnerable to speculation.

### Disadvantages

> Unable to set interest rates freely as must adjust them to keep exchange rate fixed.

> Government need to hold large reserves of gold and foreign currency which is expensive.

> The rate which is fixed may be inappropriate and cause trade deficits (less exports than imports), less growth and more unemployment.

# Floating Exchange Rates

When the government does not intervene in the setting of exchange rates, but allows the value of a currency to be determined by the price mechanism (demand and supply).

## Advantages

➢ Balance of Trade can be helped since currency can freely fall, and this may help improve employment in export industries.

➢ No need to hold lots of foreign currency reserves.

➢ Control over interest rates and monetary policy for other economic objectives like controlling inflation.

## Disadvantages

➢ Currency fluctuations cause uncertainty for international trade and business and encourages speculation.

➢ Possibility of protectionist measures and trade barriers being used to correct exchange rate movements.

# Managed Exchange Rates (Dirty float)

Between 1967 and 1992, sterling was in a number of managed exchange rates.

These allow a currency to float but within specified limits. When the currency nears the upper or lower limits the government will intervene.

One of the most famous managed exchange rate was the Exchange Rate Mechanism (ERM).

Currently 43% of currencies in the world operate some managed exchange rate system.

# MULTINATIONALS

An organisation with a headquarters in one country and who operates in 2 or more countries.

Multinationals with a head office in the UK are usually Public Limited Companies (PLC).

## Factors multinationals may consider when choosing location

### Locating in a Developing Country

> ➢ Lower wages.

> ➢ Lower tax rates.

> ➢ Plenty land at cheap prices.

> ➢ Government grants given.

> ➢ Less likely to be trade unions in place.

> ➢ Large population of available workers.

### Locating in Scotland

> ➢ EU member.

> ➢ Good education standards so productivity high.

> ➢ English spoken which is main business language.

> ➢ Political stability.

> ➢ Good infrastructure.

# Effects of multinationals on host country

## Positive effects

- ➤ Create jobs.

- ➤ Increases tax revenue from employees.

- ➤ Introduce new management techniques.

## Negative effects

- ➤ Can have too much influence on a government.

- ➤ Profits go back to home country of multinationals origin.

- ➤ Can move from a country when any grant conditions finish.

- ➤ Uses up natural resources.

- ➤ Senior jobs tend to go to people from home country of multinational.

# Advantages of becoming a multinational

> Allows organisations to increase customers and sales which should increase profits.

> Allows organisations to take advantage of economies of scale (savings made by larger businesses) and reduce costs of products.

> Allow organisations to employ cheaper staff around the world and reduce costs.

> May be given grants from governments to locate in a country.

> Become larger which may result in a business being safer from takeovers.

> Spreads risks so if a business in one country struggles one in another country will not be affected.

# Disadvantages of becoming a multinational

> Legislation will be different in all countries which means extra costs to comply with them all.

> Cultural differences will mean that organisations have to be aware and sensitive of different cultures, religious beliefs and views.

> Different languages will exist and this may mean increase costs for translators or language training.

# DEVELOPING AND EMERGING ECONOMIES

In economics various groups of countries are classified under different names:-

➢ Developed countries – group of rich industrialised nations also called more developed countries (MDCs) e.g. countries in Western Europe, North America, Australasia and Japan.

➢ Developing countries – large group of poor countries in Asia, Africa and Latin America. These countries were called Third World countries and also less developed countries (LDCs).

➢ Another group are classified as emerging economies e.g. Hong Kong, Malaysia, Thailand, South Korea.

➢ Recent term BRICS has been created for a group of fast growing emerging economies: Brazil, Russia, India, China, and South Africa.

## Characteristics of Developing Countries

➢ Poverty – over ¾ of the world's population have incomes lower than those in the first world. There are however a small group of rich people.

➢ High population growth – birth rates and death rates are higher than most developed nations.

➢ High dependence on 1 or 2 exports – these are usually primary products.

➢ Agricultural Dominance – around 70% of the population in LDCs live off the land. They have subsistence level economies.

➢ Unemployment and underemployment – rural areas have underemployment due to the seasonal nature of the work.

➢ Lack of infrastructure – shortage of good roads, schools, railways, airports which are vital to economic development.

# Characteristics of Emerging Economies

➢ High economic growth rates.

➢ Rising export sales.

➢ Little reliance on agriculture – most of the production is now in manufactured goods.

➢ Rising standards of living.

➢ Increasing levels of education and training.

➢ Improving infrastructure.

# Effects of Emerging Economies on UK

## Positive effects

➢ UK firms: demand for UK products from emerging economies can present sales opportunities for UK firms. As a result, UK exports will increase and UK businesses will increase their sales and profits.

➢ UK economy: emerging economies who buy from UK help to increase employment in the UK as firms demand more workers. This helps improve the UK current account through increased exports.

## Negative effects

➢ UK firms: increased competition for UK firms because imported goods are cheaper.

➢ UK economy: increased deficit in the trade balance as the value of imports is greater than the value of exports.

# INTERNATIONAL AID/ASSISTANCE

## Motives for Giving Aid/Assistance

- Humanitarian – to help those in need. Normally foodstuffs, medicine.

- Political – to help countries sharing similar views.

- Economic – if developing countries become more productive and prosperous they will be able to contribute more to the world economy and provide new markets to sell to and reduce chance of migration issues.

## Disadvantages of Aid/Assistance

- It may not reach those in need - Corrupt governments can intercept the assistance.

- Donors may finance the capital expenditure e.g. new roads but not support the current expenditure e.g. repairs and maintenance making the resource unusable.

- Tied aid forces developing countries to buy equipment from the donor when it could be cheaper to borrow and look for a cheaper supplier.

- Aid can lead to developing countries being dependent on rich countries and give no incentive to grow from its own resources.

- Food aid can destroy local farmers if it drives the prices down.

# Types of Aid/Assistance

➢ Gifts of foodstuffs and medical aid – giving a country suitable medicines, health care and health care workers.

➢ Grants - don't need to be repaid and can be used for any reason.  Due to corruption in many LDCs there is a reluctance to give grants.

➢ Soft Loans- Loans are sometimes given with interest rates below commercial rates.

➢ Writing off debt – the US and UK have written off debts of certain countries on the condition that the money saved is used to relieve poverty.

➢ Tied aid – this is grants or loans that need to be used to purchase equipment from the donor country.

# Effects of Aid/Assistance

➢ Loans/grants can in the long term increase the incomes of developing countries and so enable them to achieve greater economic growth.

➢ Sending specialists to give advice can result in the developing country engaging in more trade with other countries.

➢ Giving suitable medical aid improves the life expectancy of the country's inhabitants so they can become more productive.

# THE EUROPEAN UNION (EU)

## History of the EU

The EU started as 6 countries and was called the European Coal and Steel Community (ECSC). It has enlarged at various points to now have 28 members with the biggest single increase taking place in 2004.

The name has changed a few times from the original to the European Economic Community (EEC), then the European Community (EC) before the current name.

In a referendum held in June 2016 the UK voted to leave and the process of making this happen, known as Brexit, is continuing as this guide was being written.

### Dates Joined

1958 - Belgium, France, Germany, Italy, Luxembourg, Netherlands.

1973 - Denmark, Ireland, UK.

1981 - Greece.

1986 - Spain, Portugal.

1995 - Finland, Sweden, Austria.

2004 - Cyprus, Czech Rep, Estonia, Hungary, Latvia, Lithuania, Malta, Poland, Slovak Rep, Slovenia.

2007 - Romania, Bulgaria.

2013 - Croatia.

The EU has created a single market.

A single market has 3 key features:

> A free trade area – free movement of goods and services.

> A customs union – COMMON EXTERNAL TARIFF – all member nations must impose the same trade barriers on non-member countries.

> A single factor market – free movement of labour (people).

## Advantages of EU Membership/ Single Market

> Creates more trade with the removal of trade barriers.

> Economies of scale can be gained by businesses as the size of the market has increased hugely.

> Greater choice for consumers and more employment opportunities.

> Competition has increased which leads to more efficient use of resources and more innovation.

> Regulations and standards are the same in all countries guaranteeing safety.

> Movement (mobility) of resources has allowed labour and capital to locate where they may be efficiently employed.

# Disadvantages of EU Membership/Single Market

➢ Common external tariff has diverted trade away from the entire EU.

➢ Firms have moved to the more prosperous areas of the EU which has widened the gap between the rich and poor regions.

# Other issues/tensions between EU member countries

➢ VAT – variations in VAT rates between countries which can distort prices.

➢ Differences in Excise Duties – alcohol and petrol are cheaper in some EU countries than others.

➢ Different tax rates on company profits – e.g. Ireland has a lower corporation tax level making it successful in attracting investment over other members who rates are higher.

➢ Lower wages available in some EU economies compared to others.

➢ Migration issues to and from EU countries – many people moving from countries in Eastern Europe to those in Western Europe but few people moving the other way. This has caused tensions amongst resident population particularly those seeking work and has placed increased demands on education and health services.

➢ Deciding how much should be contributed by each member to the EU Budget.

➢ Differences in language, culture and current size make the organisation difficult to run and decisions to be made.

➢ Adoption of the single currency (the Euro) by only some members has created two levels within the EU.

# INTERNATIONAL TRADING AND MONETARY ORGANISATIONS

## World Trade Organisation

➤ The World Trade Organisation was formed in 1995 and replaced the General Agreement on Tariffs and Trade (GATT).

➤ Encourages free trade by reducing tariffs and other trade barriers.

➤ Mediates in trade disputes.

➤ Ensures member countries comply with trade agreements – can impose penalties.

## International Monetary Fund

➤ Encourages the growth of world trade.

➤ Helps members facing currency collapses.

➤ Offers assistance on economic matters.

➤ Provides loans to national governments (especially developing countries).

➤ Encourages moves to market economies away from government ownership.

➤ Holds regular meetings to discuss world monetary problems.

➤ Provides help to countries experiencing debt crises.

# World Bank

- ➤ The full name for the World Bank is the International Bank for Reconstruction and Development (IBRD)

- ➤ Set up at the same time as the International Monetary Fund.

- ➤ The World Bank provides long-term assistance for development.

- ➤ Largest source of multilateral aid.

- ➤ Member states contribute funds in proportion to their national income.

- ➤ Gives loans to LDCs. Previously it was only for development of infrastructure but now targeting projects that relieve poverty e.g. healthcare and education.

# ACTIVITIES

## Research Task 1 - Trade Barriers

Carry out research and then prepare a report giving details of the embargo of Scottish haggis in the US.

Include dates, reasons and impacts.

## Research Task 2 - Trade Barriers

Use www.bbc.co.uk/news and search on each of the following trade barriers – quota, embargo and tariff.

Choose one story on each of the trade barriers and summarise the content.

## Research Task 3 - Trade Barriers

Research the connection between the creation of the soft drink Fanta and trade barriers.

## Research Task 4 - Exchange Rate Systems

Research and record 2 current examples of the use of a fixed exchange rate system – include the countries and currencies involved, when the fixed rate was introduced and what it is set at.

Research and record 2 current examples of the use of a managed (dirty float) exchange rate system – include the countries and currencies involved, when the managed rate was introduced and what the upper and lower limits are.

## Research Task 5 - Exchange Rate Mechanism

Create a newspaper article on the Exchange Rate Mechanism – when it existed, what it was, why it ended.

# Research Task 6 - Exchange Rate Speculation

Prepare a report on George Soros and how he made money from exchange rate speculation in 1992 in the UK and in 1997 in Thailand.

# Research Task 7 - Foreign Direct Investment

Using either BBC or google news websites, search Foreign Direct Investment. Research 2 recent news stories on this area.

Mention the companies and countries, what the investment is, the amounts of money and any other interesting information.

# Research Task 8 - Multinationals

Choose any non UK multinational to research.

Provide a company profile - location of HQ, what the business does, current chief executive, how many countries it operates in, how many staff it employs in each country and any other interesting information.

# Research Task 9 - World Trade Organisation (WTO)

1.    When did the WTO start?

2.    What was the previous name of the WTO?

3.    Who is the current Director General?

4.    How many members does the WTO currently have?

5.    Where are the WTO headquarters?

# Research Task 10 - The International Monetary Fund (IMF)

1.    How many member countries does the IMF currently have?

2.    Where and when was the idea for the IMF conceived?

3.    How is the IMF funded?

# Research Task 11 - The World Bank

1.    Where is the World Bank based?

2.    When was the World Bank founded?

3.    Who is the current President of the World Bank?

# Short Revision Questions

1   Describe International Trade. (1)

2   Suggest the main difference between Comparative and Absolute Advantage. (2)

3   Give 3 reasons for trade protection. (3)

4   Give 3 examples of Protectionism/Trade Barriers. (3)

5   Name the two sections of the Balance of Payments Account. (2)

6   Give 2 components within each section of the Balance of Payments (2)

7   State what FDI stands for. (1)

8   Define an exchange rate. (1)

9   Give 2 factors which can change the exchange rate. (2)

10  Describe the difference between a floating and a fixed exchange rate. (1)

# EXAM STYLE QUESTIONS

1.      Describe what is meant by an embargo. (2)

2.      Describe 3 components of the current account of the UK Balance of payments. (3)

3.      Describe features of the European Union. (3)

4.      Explain the benefits of free trade to an economy. (3)

5.      Explain the benefits to a developing country of hosting a multinational company. (3)

6.      Explain factors that may decrease demand for sterling on foreign exchange markets. (2)

# Suggested Solutions – Research Tasks

## Research Task 9 - World Trade Organisation (WTO)

1. When did the WTO start? – 1995.

2. What was the previous name of the WTO? – General Agreement on Tariffs and Trade (GATT).

3. Who is the current Director General? – Ngozi Okonjo-Iweala (at Mar 21).

4. How many members does the WTO currently have? - 164.

5. Where are the WTO headquarters? – Geneva, Switzerland.

## Research Task 10 - The International Monetary Fund (IMF)

1. How many member countries does the IMF currently have? – 190. (at Mar 2021)

2. Where and when was the idea for the IMF conceived? – Bretton Woods conference in 1944.

3. How is the IMF funded? – Member countries pay subscriptions.

## Research Task 11 - The World Bank

1. Where is the World Bank based? – Washington D.C., USA

2. When was the World Bank founded? – July 1945

3. Who is the current President of the World Bank? – David Malpass (Dec 2019)

# Short Revision Questions – Suggested Solutions

1.  Describe International Trade. (1) – Buying and selling of goods and services between people and business located in different countries

2.  Suggest the main difference between Comparative and Absolute Advantage. (2) – With absolute advantage each country is better at producing a product and they should focus on that solely and trade whereas with comparative advantage a country may be better at producing a number of products but should still focus only on the one product with the lowest opportunity cost and look to trade.

3.  Give 3 reasons for trade protection. (3) - Protect jobs, protect industries important to a country, for political reasons, retaliating against trade barriers imposed by other countries

4.  Give 3 examples of Protectionism/Trade Barriers. (3)

5.  Name the two sections of the Balance of Payments Account. (2) – Current Account and Capital Account

6.  Give 2 components within each section of the Balance of Payments (2) – Current Account – Balance of Trade in Goods, Balance of Trade in Services, Net Investment Income, Transfers. Capital Account – Foreign Direct Investment, Direct Portfolio Investment, Movements of Income, Hot money flows.

7.  State what FDI stands for. (1) – Foreign Direct Investment

8.  Define an exchange rate. (1) – the value of a one currency when converted into another

9.  Give 2 factors which can change the exchange rate. (2) – Interest Rates, Inflation, Speculation, Imports and Export demands, Levels of tourism

10. Describe the difference between a floating and a fixed exchange rate. (1) – A fixed exchange rate does not move and is set by a government who maintain the rate s whereas a floating exchange rate is set by the forces of demand and supply and moves constantly.

# Exam Style Questions – Suggested Solutions

1.     Describe what is meant by an embargo. (2)

An embargo is a complete ban on trade with a particular country or for a particular product. (1) For example, haggis from Scotland has been banned in the USA for safety reasons since the early 1970s. (1)

2.     Describe 3 components of the current account of the UK Balance of payments. (3)

Components of the current account of the Balance of Payments include:

Balance of Trade in Goods - the export and import of manufactured goods (1) e.g.  Whisky and cars (1)

Balance of Trade in Services - the export and import of services (1) e.g. banking, transport, insurance, tourism. 1)

Net Investment Income - Interest, profits and dividends received on UK investments overseas less interest, profits and dividends paid to foreigners investing in the UK. (1)

Transfers - Payments and receipts to and from the UK government and the EU, international organisations and aid (1) (usually a deficit). (1)

3.     Describe features of the European Union. (3)

Features of the European Union include:

A free trade area – free movement of goods and services between member countries (1) i.e. no trade barriers like quotas, tariffs or embargos. (1)

A customs union – COMMON EXTERNAL TARIFF – all member nations must impose the same trade barriers on non-member countries. (1)

A single factor market – free movement of labour (people) between member countries without any visa or other entry restrictions. (1)

4.    Explain the benefits of free trade to an economy. (3)

Free trade offers consumers more variety in the types of goods and services they purchase which improves their quality of life. (1)

Free trade allows goods to enter a country without trade barriers so the goods are cheaper in price. (1)

Free trade provides competition to domestic businesses which results in them producing high quality goods. (1)

Removes the threat of retaliation from other countries which helps reduce international conflicts. (1)

Increases the volume of world trade and this leads to a higher level of world output. (1)

5.    Explain the benefits to a developing country of hosting a multinational company. (3)

Create jobs which should increase economic growth. (1)

Increases tax revenue from employees which government can then spend on services like education and health. (1)

Introduces new management techniques which leads to improved quality. (1)

6.    Explain factors that may decrease demand for sterling on foreign exchange markets. (2)

If UK interest rates fall relative to elsewhere, it will become less attractive to deposit money in the UK and demand for sterling will reduce leading to hot money outflows. (1)

If inflation in the UK is higher than elsewhere, then UK exports will become less competitive and there will be a decrease in demand for Pound Sterling as less demand to buy UK goods. (1)

A decrease in demand for UK goods and services abroad (exports) will decrease demand for pound sterling. (1)

A decrease in people visiting the UK will decrease demand for pound sterling. (1)

Printed in Great Britain
by Amazon

16734934R00090